Words of Caring Meant for Sharing

by
Mary Lee Cunningham

Copyright © 2023, Mary Lee Cunningham
Second Edition
All rights reserved.
ISBN: 979-8-9855041-4-9

 Publisher, Mary Lee Cunningham under supervision of Scotchwood Hill Publishing Services

DEDICATION

I dedicate this volume to
sad people,
hurting people,
and happy people -
all of whom I pray will be
blessed by these words and images
stirred by God's own Spirit.

ACKNOWLEDGEMENTS

While I have not used scripture citations within my poems, essays, or the accompanying notes, I trust the reader will discover the handprint of God within each entry. As such, it is to Him I owe my greatest thanks. In addition, I wish to express my sincere gratitude to the following people who have helped me complete the labor of love you now hold in your hands.

~~~

PATRICIA CLARK BLAKE – Thanks, for being not only a dear friend but also the "burr under my saddle," *yet not in a bad way*! Without your continual encouragement and reassurance this book would never have become a reality.

MARTHA RODRIGUEZ – How could I ever have gotten this laid out and ready for printing without your skilled assistance? Your attention to detail and suggestions in regard to arrangement of the cover, etc., was so helpful.

SANET LEE JENNINGS – Thank you for scouring my introductory remarks to make sure they flowed smoothly and communicated my meanings.

DIETLINDE SPEARS - Your editing after the first printing was invaluable, dear friend. Thank you so very much.

WRITERS INK OF NORTHEAST ARKANSAS – I am grateful for each of the talented writers in this group who kept telling me I had material deserving to be published.

SCORES OF OTHER FRIENDS – I cannot name all my other friends who have so often told me after they read or received one of my poems as a gift, "You need to write a book!" I'm glad my words blessed each of you, and I hope this collection will bless others who may read it.

People sometimes ask, "Where do you get the inspiration for your poems?" Here is the answer I typically offer. "Often, I will awaken with a thought or idea I need to write down. Then the words simply pour onto the page. However, if I do not act promptly, they can disappear—never coming to mind again." When it's commissioned poems I'm writing, I work from extensive questionnaires. These poems seem to fits so perfectly one recipient remarked, "It's like you've been reading my mail!" I hope some of what follows on these pages will resonate with you.

Mary Lee

My Inspiration

God knew before I came to be
how long I would get to live.
He knew what sorrows I would face,
and what gift to me He'd give.

My gift is writing thoughts in verse
to express what's in my heart.
Those deep emotions trapped inside
can almost tear me apart.

The thoughts I share in poetry
typically come out as rhymes.
This style no longer is in vogue,
as it was in olden times.

When I've shared my poems with others,
"That's me!" friends often would say.
I learned my poems weren't just for me
but were meant to give away.

Everyone goes through some hard times,
with losses, sadness, and grief.
Many can't seem to find the words
to bring them peace and relief.

"Expressions from the Heart" I write
do not really come from me.
God touches my heart, and I write.
So, He's the author, you see.

TABLE OF CONTENTS

<u>Section 1</u>   Pages 1-18

God's Perfect Design:

Relating to God & His Plans for Man

<u>Section 2</u>   Pages 19-39

Relationships:

Friendships – Marriage – Divorce

Section 3   Pages 40-67

Family Issues Through the Seasons:

Parents – Children – Aging Parents - Dementia

Section 4   Pages 68-94

Personal Struggles:

Physical – Emotional – Spiritual - Addiction

Section 5   Pages 95-117

End of Life Issues:

Anticipating Death – Death – Dealing with Grief

Section 6   Pages 118-145

Odds & Ends:

Memories & A Touch of Humor

GOD'S PERFECT DESIGN:
Relating to God & His Plans for Man

God's Design

Our Father created each of us
with something that makes us unique.
Far too often we worry and fret
and we think of ourselves as weak.

Yet, how can a person who's caring –
quick to bless everyone she knows –
not be seen as a valuable gem
because of the kindness she shows?

If you begin to put yourself down –
and think of your talents are few –
consider what you've received from God
and work He's entrusted to you.

On tasks you're given, do your best.
Fulfill them like God had in mind.
Then as you work, using all your skills,
an increase in self-worth you'll find.

Back in the 1960's traditional roles for women were being ridiculed and spoken of with disdain by prominent women in the culture. The women who identified themselves as stay-at-home-moms and homemakers were pressured to pursue **more important** callings in society and the corporate world. Yet, in reality, being a full-time keeper in the home is a role in which one should take pride. In fact, it is perhaps **the most important** role any woman can have, and doing it well can bring honor to one's husband, to her family, and to God! *Mary Lee*

This poem reminds us of our need to not only see God in the good and pleasant things in life, but also to realize His hand works in those things which do *not* appear to be good or are unpleasant. I first shared this poem with Diane and Jim Medlock when his health was failing and his days on earth were growing fewer. Both of them were strong in their faith and in their love for each other. That love and their faith was magnified as they together went through Jim's lasts days on this earth. They KNEW that even in that, God was still caring for them. *Mary Lee*

To See God

To see God in a new sunrise
and in a bright sunset, too,
Neither of these is difficult.
They're something we all can do.

We see God in a smiling child
who is both tender and sweet,
or when we unite with old friends
who we're happy to meet.

We thank God when He's providing
our food, or shelter or wealth.
At times such as these it's easy,
but what if we're in poor health?

Seeing God THEN is a factor
of someone's genuine trust.
The world calls this impossible,
but love tells us that we must.

In the hard times when we see God
and affirm His love is true –
this truly says you trust in God
and know that he'll take care you.

Look for the *RAINBOW!*

When the world tries to steal my joy –
when my faith is growing cold –
help me, Lord, to remember You
and Your promises of old.

You once hung in the sky of blue
a reminder we could see,
and when great sorrows flood my soul,
the rainbow is there for me.

It says one day the rains will cease –
and the sun will shine anew,
but more than this it also tells
of the love I have from You!

To the age-old promise may I cling
as affirmed by the bright rainbow.
It's *real meaning* is important,
a truth all people should know!

In decades past, the story of the Great Flood always thrilled children in Bible classes. It told of the building of the ark, the gathering of the animals by twos, and the flood that covered the entire earth! Yet, Noah, his family, and all the animals were kept safe inside the Ark because they <u>believed</u> and <u>obeyed</u> God. We learned how God orchestrated all the events to bring salvation to Noah and his family. The <u>rainbow</u> was significant then **and** now. God gave it as a sign to remind Himself and mankind of His promise to never destroy the earth again with a flood. It's important for new generations to learn the **true** meaning of the rainbow and about how we too must honor and obey His Word to receive the salvation He offers.

Mary Lee

Have you noticed how there is often a correlation between how a day gets started and how it ends? When we begin our day taking time for God rather than with worrying about the long To Do List waiting for us, it will generally go much more smoothly. Furthermore, the end of the day will typically be much sweeter and more satisfying, too. Give it a try and see how it works for you! *Mary Lee*

A Good Start for the Day

It's tempting to hit the ground running
when my *"To Do"* list is so long.
By taking time for God at the start,
He will put in my heart a song.

It may be a song of gratitude -
one that's overflowing with praise,
or it may be one to bring me peace
if it looks like *"one of those days"*.

Each day if I'll be still and listen,
bits of truth He will let me see.
If I follow the course He gives me,
then more like His Son I will be.

God knows everything that awaits me,
before my bare feet hit the floor.
What I learn in our time together
is not to fear what lies in store.

How great is the Lord God of Glory
who cares for me every day!
I'm thankful He's shared His Word with me
and that He hears me when I pray.

Whatever the tasks I must tackle,
I'll not have to do them alone.
May I start my day with thankfulness
since He calls me one of His own.

Have you ever felt *BUSY* – *RUSHED* – *STRESSED*?

Of course, you have. All of us know what it is like because it's a common complaint of man, especially in this fast-paced world. In fact, society even seems to promote it! Some reasons we find ourselves in such a state is because of our tendency to become over-extended, overcommitted, and over-worked. In this poem I am specifically addressing challenges many women face, though men are susceptible to their own pressures and challenges. The admonition I offer fits everyone. May we all seek to consider and use our time with care and gratitude because it is truly a gift from God.

Mary Lee

What Shall I Do?

Are you pulled in many directions,
and you can't decide what to do?
Should you first clean the bathroom toilets,
or just take the kids to the zoo?

Should you go to another meeting
or attend some social affair?
Should you take a walk to clear your head
as you breathe in God's clean, fresh air?

Should you sit down beside your husband
when the laundry needs to be done,
or should you make plans for vacation
where you can just lounge in the sun?

When life seems to be much too hectic,
and you need a refreshing break,
find time alone for just you and God.
What a difference that time can make!

It can help you relieve the pressures
so you can know what you should do.
You'll realize God is so awesome,
and you'll marvel that He loves you.

Yes, the gift of time is quite precious!
On what or on whom is yours spent?
With the time you've chosen to give God,
what message to Him have you sent?

Each moment we have is a present.
Take care how you give time away.
Making God your first priority,
ensures you a much better day!

A common concern of many people, even those who have been Christians for decades, is "Have I done enough?" Although they read God's Word; believe Jesus is God's son; and believe He died on the cross for sinners; they may still have trouble getting over the "good enough" hurdle. This is about one man's coming to terms with the reality his salvation **wasn't** based on what he does or doesn't do but on what Christ did for him. *Mary Lee*

It's Not Up to Me

As I find myself getting older,
just living at times can be tough.
I wish I had done more for others.
I hope what I did was enough.

There were people I should have talked to –
friends who didn't know of God's grace.
They had no thought when life was over,
if they'd see a smile on His face.

I'm so glad that perfection in me
isn't something my Lord demands.
He knows I'm human, with many flaws,
yet He loves me and understands.

I praise God, *it isn't up to me!*
No human can save his own soul.
Thankfully, Jesus died for my sins.
In His doing so, He made me whole.

As the end of my life draws nearer,
I'm thankful God sees me as pure.
Since I've been washed in my Savior's blood,
I rest, knowing I am secure.

This piece was written to share at a Ladies' Retreat for Ross Road Church of Christ in Memphis. The theme for the weekend was "Bloom Where You Are Planted". We were challenged to remember how we don't have to do GREAT THINGS nor a GREAT NUMBER of things in order to be pleasing to God. I hope this poem conveyed that message. *Mary Lee*

How Many *Talents* Are Needed?

May you bloom where you are planted,
And then in God's service grow!
Using your God-given talents,
may your worth you come to know.

Many people don't understand
the joy in serving others.
Instead, they're seeking to <u>be</u> served
by their sisters and brothers.

But those who are the happiest –
the ones who feel most content –
are people who lift others' loads,
for this is our Lord's intent.

Though your deeds may not seem so grand
when measured by earthly gauge,
it's God who weighs your performance.
for you're acting on His stage!

So, if "but a cup of water"
into your hands He's given,
it's how you use your *single gift*
that counts with God in Heaven.

"As you did it unto the least . . .
then you did it unto me."
May each of us now understand,
it's only <u>one</u> gift we need.

It must be difficult to be a man today or to be raising boys. I wrote this as I considered what I believe is a crisis in our nation. Our culture seems to be methodically stripping men of their manhood and their God-ordained place in the home, family, society, and the church. I pray God will help our men to be who He intends for them to be – strong, confident, God-honoring leaders, despite the message society gives them. Also, I pray for parents to have the wisdom and strength to rear their sons to become real men who will honor God and be faithful to Him no matter what it takes. *Mary Lee*

Raising (and Being) Men as God Designed

Who'll teach our boys how they can be men
and follow the pattern God gave?
Men who'll honor the Father above
and lead so their families they'll save.

Though the world has been redefining
what a man and leader should be,
God says he'll protect his family
as he lives with integrity.

A real man doesn't bully or shout
so others by him will be heard.
It's for his kindness and character,
folks listen, respecting his word.

A real man knows he isn't perfect,
and this he will freely admit.
He will ask others for forgiveness,
and bad habits, he'll work to quit.

No, a real man's role isn't easy,
and hard calls he often must make.
In making them he'll seek God's wisdom,
and pray he'll not make a mistake.

God bless all you men who'll embrace this.
(God help those who do not as well.)
Be strong, be brave, and courageous men,
so in you, God's Spirit will dwell.

God's creation is beautiful in all seasons, and taking time to study it can yield powerful faith lessons. On this winter day, I was drawn to take a photo of the bare tree branches behind my home. It was easy to see the sky through them. The twists and turns of the branches as described in the poem are clearly visible without the thick foliage of summer. Let me encourage you as you observe simple things in nature to think of how they proclaim the majesty of God. *Mary Lee*

Twists & Turns in Trees and Me

There is a special beauty in bare trees in winter.
During this season, the shape of each branch is
exposed with all its twists, turns, and tangles.

> At times, **we** may feel like our lives are as gnarled and knotted as tree branches exposed in the dead of winter, but do not despair or lose heart.

>> It is natural for tree branches to go this way and that as they grow, for they are on a quest to find the light.

>>> In a similar fashion, we Christians will often make *course corrections* in our lives, yet we should not let these discourage us.

>>> We must recognize that in making these correction we are seeking to draw closer to the True Light—our Lord and Savior.

>>>> And this, dear friend, is exactly what our Heavenly Father desires for us to do.

The desire for pretty lawns seems to be an important thing in the neighborhood where I live. Landscaping companies do a brisk business all year round, but especially in Spring when those pesky weeds start popping up everywhere. One year I must have pulled out a bushel basket full as I tried to get rid of them, but they just kept coming back. I eventually sought professional help. Even then, it was not an easy task. This appears to have a parallel in removing sins from our lives. Do you sometimes find your life needs some weeding like mine?   *Mary Lee*

Is It Time for Weeding?

The spring rains now are falling,
watering all the weeds.
How dearly their removal
my green and brown lawn needs!

The weeds grow very quickly,
popping up all around,
I fear they're like *little sins*
that in my life are found.

God, help me pluck pesky sins,
lest they quickly take control
and ruin my witness for Jesus
and do harm to my soul.

Please, weed me as is needed
so, I'll look good for You.
Then I'll reflect Your beauty
the way that I should do.

> Have you ever allowed yourself to get caught up in worrying about the future? After all, our country seems to be in a mess as it casts aside the principles first laid down by our Forefathers – many of which were principles found in God's Word. Personally, we may be struggling to figure out what our own future will look like. Read the following words and find encouragement in the truths they proclaim.
>
> *Mary Lee*

Not Unknown to God

Where you are today
and where you will be tomorrow
are not unknown to God.
Trust Him.

Even when you are fearful of the future,
believe He has a plan for your life.
He is orchestrating all the details of it
so that as they unfold, you will be blessed.

This world's problems and its systems
will one day disappear for they are not eternal.
God's will is.

One day you will discover all the wonderful things
God has prepared just for you
because you are His child.

So, take heart!
Even if you don't know the future,
you know the One who orchestrates it,
and He loves you with an everlasting love!

The God of Creation knew all there was to know about the things He created — the animals, birds, sea creatures, and also humans. Part of what He designed into each lifeform was how He intended for them to procreate and multiply. Somewhere along the way, mankind determined they knew better than God how things should work. May the poem below provide some food for thought on the subject. *Mary Lee*

Two Jacks, Two Jills or God's Design

The birds hear a cacophony
as spring is well underway.
Fat worms tunnel beneath the ground
as insects buzz, crawl, and play.

God, the Creator, made them all,
ordering how they'd survive;
how they would mate and procreate
in order to live and thrive.

Mankind was made by God's design,
the male then his female mate.
Coming together they formed one,
and each one's passions they'd sate.

When man chose to bend God's design,
no children by this means came.
Though couples called themselves *married*,
to God, it was not the same

Marriage was planned to bless mankind.
Through it, the whole earth He'd fill.
This couldn't happen if couples
contained two "Jacks" or two "Jills".

Such perversions God will not bless.
Sodom's example is clear.
For those who choose this way of life,
His wrath will one day appear.

No one desires destruction of
friends who in that life are caught.
For this reason, the truths of God
with tenderness must be taught.

Forgiveness for all kinds of sins,
was paid for at Calvary.
This sacrifice by God's own Son
was offered for you and me!

May God open hearts and the eyes
of those who've believed the lie.
Pure and holy lives we must live.
So, t'ward this end may we try.

How wonderful it is to live in this beautiful world God created! For many of us who live in a region that has four distinct seasons, we find our world continually changing color when each new one gets underway. To illustrate some of nature's beauty I am sharing the photo of some beautiful trees from the yard of friends, Rebecca & Kenneth Ryan. *Mary Lee*

OUR CHANGING WORLD AND ITS BEAUTIFUL COLORS

Each year after the summer
has given way to fall,
the changes in the landscape
are witnessed by us all.

The first thing that we'll notice,
many greens disappear
as the warm colors of fall
gradually will appear.

Though those won't be here for long,
since chilly turns to cold.
How we will miss the beauty
of orange, red, and gold.

When the foliage disappears
from every hardwood tree,
Then bare limbs and branches
are what we'll get to see.

Yet, within that starkness
beauty still doesn't end.
Before long comes the springtime
when colors God will send!

*What an Extraordinary Artist
is our God who colors each season
so beautifully!*

He Paid Our Sin Debt

God had a special plan in His mind
even before earth was made.
Jesus knew He would come to earth,
though with God, He could have stayed.

Since man was blessed a with free will,
he'd need to be shown the way
he could gain forgiveness of sins,
for his debt, he could not pay.

Into the world our Savior came
so He could save souls of man.
He entered into grief and woe
for this would fulfil God's plan.

Friendships untrue, insults and pain,
the sorrow of seeing friends die -
Jesus witnessed each one of these
before ascending on high.

"Why would He do it?" some might ask.
Just one reason can there be.
He did it to prove God's dear love
for the lost, like you and me.

None of us like to be in debt. Once in it, getting out can be hard and costly. However, getting out of our debt for sin would be **impossible** were it not for Jesus. God knew this, and He had a plan to wipe out man's sin debt. It too was costly. In fact, it cost Jesus His very life! How can we thank Him enough for this wonderful gift of love?   *Mary Lee*

RELATIONSHIPS:
Friendships, Marriage & Divorce

As you read this poem, think of all the friends you've had through the years and the impact each one made on your life. Perhaps consider next the impact you may have had on them. Hopefully, the recollections of both will be positive. Let us treasure our friendships —old and new for they are indeed a gift. *Mary Lee*

The Gift of Friendship

To have a good friend is a true gift.
Some people seem to have many.
Others there are who go through life
and sadly, do not have any.

Yes, people will change as time goes by,
and we each have bad times and good.
We grieve in deaths, and rejoice in births,
and we'd alter some things if we could.

True friendships we keep throughout the years
and distance that keeps us apart.
The secret that makes this possible
is friendship remains in our heart.

Friends we've kept through the seasons of life
shine brightly like stars in the skies.
Let us thank God for sending each one.
Forever, these friends let us prize.

In our busy, sometimes chaotic world, many Christians often question whether their lives have meaning. They work their forty or fifty-plus hours each week and come home spent. They want to be doing more for the Lord, but when work is so demanding and time-consuming they don't see how they can. Besides, many also have family responsibilities as well as work. When the end of a day comes, they just want to collapse. They know morning will arrive all too soon, and they must be "up and at 'um" — ready to begin again.

I have a Christian friend, Mary Lynn Woodruff, who often felt such discouragements. I sent her a note with the words below to remind her that what she does, *DOES* make a difference in the lives of many. It's how she represents her Lord in her everyday life! If you ever get a chance to meet her, I have no doubt you will be blessed.

Consider how could YOU bless someone today? *Mary Lee*

My Friend, You Make a Difference

Dear Mary Lynn,

I'm writing to share with you the beautiful and truthful comments I recently heard **about you** from Rise Rothe. She told about having been shopping at Dillard's one day when she saw you *in action*. No, it wasn't you doing someone's makeup or ringing up a sale. It was you spreading your *"Special Mary Lynn Sunshine"* to people who passed by. She said you seemed to know EVERYONE by name and you gave each of them a warm smile and a greeting that they gladly received and returned. Rise said it was so obvious that you were an *Ambassador for the Lord* sharing His love as you went about your work right there at the cosmetic counter!

Hearing that about you warmed my heart. Never forget, dear sister, THAT is exactly what our heavenly Father wants all of us to do — to **be Jesus** to others as we go on our way each day!

Thanks, Mary Lynn, for your good example. ♥ *Mary Lee*

> By the time each of us started kindergarten we had begun to learn how having friends was a neat thing. If you were reared in a family where you had siblings, you already had your first introduction to friendship. I remember an old Coca-Cola slogan from my youth. It affirmed, "Things go better with Coke!" I think a great slogan for humanity would be " Life goes better with friends!" *Mary Lee*

Friendship Secret

In ways, this world is a lonely place,
and friends, we desire and we need.
If you've been wanting to find a friend,
Then to these words you might take heed.

<u>What</u> is the true secret of friendship,
and <u>How</u> do you make friendships grow?
<u>When</u> you so much want to find a friend,
<u>Where's</u> the first place you should go?

Try looking at people around you -
the ones who you see every day.
It is likely among that number,
a friend you just might find today.

So many around you are lonely,
and perhaps they don't have a clue.
Take a chance and say, "Hi! How are you?"
You might find a new friend *or two*!

Raymond and Dietlindé Spears are very dear friends I met when we were stationed with the U.S. Air Force at Hahn AB, Germany. While there, Dietlindé and I frequently enjoyed going out for cake, coffee, and conversations. Upon moving back to the States, we didn't live close enough to have many such outings. So, I wrote this poem for her in hopes that we could take a "trip together in our minds," even if it wasn't a literal one like Tom and Huck on their river raft. Both she and I loved the image and the little poem. Hope you will, too! *Mary Lee*

Two Friends Upon the River

To float along on a river,
like Tom Sawyer and old Huck Finn!
To let all the world slip past us -
So God's beauty we could take in!

To ponder on life's deep issues -
each weighing in with our views,
unconcerned about the weather
or what we had heard on the news!

This trip would surely be lovely,
though it's doubtful we'll take that ride
letting ourselves relax and dream
of the things we have never tried.

At least as we read this poem,
in our minds we enjoyed a cruise,
and that break from all life's pressures
was a 'trip' that we both could use!

Although it isn't intentional, we sometimes fail to take time to honor friendships that are dear to us. This is a big mistake. Some friendships may be newly made, while others may be treasured old ones. This poem was written to remind us to acknowledge and give thanks for our friends. Because friendships are SO IMPORTANT, even when it isn't a friend's birthday, if you drop them a note, send a text, or give them a call, it can mean you so much. These things can help keep the fires of friendship glowing brightly. *Mary Lee*

A Poem for Your Birthday
or
"In Appreciation of Our Friendship"]

Our friendship is old
(but then *so are we*).
that old things are good,
I hope you'll agree.

"Old" means we've weathered
rough life storms that came.
Though our bodies aged,
inside we're the same —

the same young girls
who laughed and cried
who went to the movies
and over boys sighed.

Between then and now,
we both have been blessed.
I pray this birthday
brings you all the best!

Prospective brides (and grooms) often share loving words as they anticipate their wedding and the life they hope to build together. *[Indeed, this is the "stuff" of which poetry is made!]* During this period, everything is happy and blissful, just as they expect their marriage to be. The young woman who is the bride in this poem is indeed positive and optimistic. Perhaps a companion poem from the prospective groom would have provided a nice balance. After all, a good marriage takes two – no, make that **THREE** *for* It shouldn't leave out God! *Mary Lee*

For The Keeper of My Heart
[As a Bride-to-Be Anticipates Her Marriage]

My Love, what gift can I give you?
What kindness to you can I show –
that will convey my gratefulness
for the love you've helped me to know?

When we speak, there is communion.
It's two souls engaging as one.
We can share all of our longings
that with others we've never done.

We share the intimate secrets
that our hearts have long kept inside.
With trust we've in each other,
we have nothing that we must hide.

In becoming one in marriage,
we will walk side-by-side through life.
You I will honor and cherish
as a faithful helpmate and wife.

Though marriages do hit potholes,
and challenges, we'll surely know,
together we will seek God's will,
knowing our love He'll help to grow.

"Strange Bedfellows" is a term borrowed from Shakespeare, and it is significant when considering the backstory for these poems. The term is used when referring to a pairing of two seemingly very different people, ideologies, lifestyles, etc. These poems were some of many composed and exchanged during a relationship through the mail with a friend in prison. We began writing when his sweet mother read some of my poetry and said, "My son also writes poetry. I bet you would like his, and he would like yours." Thus, our correspondence began. We not only exchanged our own poems, but we eventually wrote some together like the two shared here. Each of us modified lines or contributed thoughts to a piece as we "danced with words", much like a couple might move

The "Dance" of the Poetic Princess and Her Prison Bard

Come close my dear love and dance near to me.
Somehow it will work, though you are not free.
While now all our dancing must be in rhyme,
we'll learn how to do it in perfect time,

.

We'll move so easily as we both sway,
waiting to hear what the other will say.
Our words will be carried over the miles
as we hope their arrival will bring smiles.

We each will create rhymes to move the heart,
and with the sweet words, love may make a start.
Before you I'll curtsy and you will bow,
for that's all the dancing we can do now.

A dance in the prison would prove too hard,
so, I'll be content with words from my bard.

together on a dance floor. As a result, the titles. Authorship for our work was attributed to an avatar we called **Lee Earl** – which is a combination of both our middle names. In addition to writing together, we also did some Bible study together through the mail.

Years later as my friend was nearing his death, he said I would never know how much our studying together had meant to him. He even said I had saved his life – something I reminded him only God could do. Still, I understood what he meant. Admittedly, I grew to love this man, but poetry was not enough upon which to build a sustainable life together post prison. *Mary Lee*

[Lee Earl 8/12/09, revised 2023]

The "Dance" Reprise

Though now, just with words, do we get to dance.
this doesn't preclude our chance for romance.
I'd prefer dancing to making a rhyme,
but I've one more year of doing hard time.

Let us in our minds try a 40's swing,
and see how much fun such "dancing" will bring?
Syllables counted for the right meter -
even some iambic pentameter.

A "boot-scooting boogie" shall we next try?
Images of that will sure makes me sigh.
People who watch us as we take the floor,
Will swear "they have often done this before!"

Though dancing with words, thus far we have done,
I hope we'll agree that it has been fun.

When two young friends were preparing to marry, I offered to write poems for them to present to their parents at the rehearsal dinner. I had expected to write two, but it turned out FOUR were required! My process in writing such poems is to ask questions, learning as much as I can about the giver and the recipient. The one below was for the mother of the groom. It required some very "creative writing" to make it appropriate for sharing since theirs had been a rather strained relationship. With some effort, I reframed some of her difficult traits so that neither she nor her son were embarrassed when they were read aloud that night. *Mary Lee*

A Poem for My Mom

Tomorrow will be my wedding day.
Some things to you, I'd like to say.
These things are rather important, too.
I'll start them off with "I love you."

I think of you Mom as so special,
and you've taught me much about life.
From you, I've learned how to be patient,
which will help both me and my wife.

Mon, you've always loved me completely,
and I know you love Missy, too.
Since this really means a lot to me,
I think it's important you knew.

I admire how you mix with people.
You can please about anyone.
You are skilled at entertaining, too,
and that's not easy to be done.

When I'm told that I have a nice smile,
do folks know I got it from you?
Yes, you always seem to be smiling,
and it really looks good on you.

So, thanks for your part in our wedding.
I'm grateful for your faith in me.
Tomorrow when I marry Missy,
I'm glad you will be there to see.

Love, Your Son

> The poem below is another I have used on a number of occasions for special couples as they were getting married. I would personalize the poem and place it in a nice frame as my wedding gift. It made me happy when some of them chose to display the poem with their wedding photos. I simply hoped it would remind them how marriage is a special gift from God—something to be treasured. *Mary Lee*

A Wedding Blessing

May all of the joys of wedded bliss
be granted to you by the Lord.
May happiness always fill your home,
and may each of you feel adored.

When life presents you with challenges,
such as those all marriages face,
always tackle them as a couple
so division won't find a place.

As you grow closer in your marriage,
it will help ensure you don't drift.
You'll come to know how sweet love can be.
(*This may be God's **second-best** gift!*)

Always stay close to one another
as you journey along life's way.
Show honor to God and to your mate,
and daily to Him jointly pray.

Consider your spouse as a treasure,
by treating them as your best friend.
Through the years your oneness will deepen
as your lives together you blend.

Thank God that you found one another.
May He give His best gifts to you.
Live with joy and harmony always,
for this keeps your love feeling new.

Marriage wasn't created **by** man, but it was created **for** man. If you are blessed to be married, do all you can to make it **the** most important relationship you are in, second only to your relationship with God. As a couple, encourage one another to be all God created each of you to be individually, applauding one another's successes and comforting your mate when they experience some disappointment or failure. If you use this approach as you go through life, your marriage will be more fulfilling for both of you and will be a testimony to the goodness of marriage as ordained by God Himself. *Mary Lee*

Married Love: Keeping the Flame Burning

Husbands, learn to show your wife kindness
through your words and in little ways.
To her they'll be sweeter than flowers,
and they'll add brightness to her days.

Sometimes, ask her out on a real date -
like the ones you'd go on before.
Remind her you think she's beautiful
and the lady whom you still adore.

Wives, often let your dear husbands hear
how safe you feel when by their side.
Let him know when he helps out at home,
to you it's a really big deal.

When either of you have a bad day
and it seems nothing has gone right,
Thank God that you have a loving spouse.
Draw them close, then hug them real tight.

Since God blessed you with one another,
now as teammates to go through your life.
Do not let pettiness interfere
for that will fill your home with strife.

Instead, make your home a safe refuge -
a place where you both are content,
for when God gave His children marriage,
this certainly was His intent.

By the time a couple has been together for fifty years, there are few things they need. So, a poem seemed like the perfect gift for my cousins, Dorcas and Hershel Wyatt, when they celebrated their 50th Wedding Anniversary several years ago. It was a simple verse, but it made them smile and added to the joy of the party. That also pleased me.

Mary Lee

In Honor of Your 50th Wedding Anniversary

When the two of you chose to marry,
you knew that your life would be grand.
It would last as long as both of you lived.
Side-by-side through the years you'd stand!

With **ten** years it started to feel real.
You both learned that life could be tough,
For good times you chose to be thankful,
as you proved you had the right stuff.

With **twenty** years down, you felt assured
and your friends told you looked good.
You still had strength to do anything,
or at least most things you once could.

When your **thirtieth** year rolled around
you knew that you should celebrate
for you'd now made for three decades
since you'd gone out on your first date!

By your **forty** year, you each had changed,
and sometimes you moved pretty slow,
but it mattered not how fast you moved,
since you had no real place to go!

On your **Fifty** year, you both knew
you'd made the right choice in one thing -
For you'd each chosen the PERFECT *ONE*
On whose finger to slip that ring!

As I wrote this poem, my life was in turmoil. My husband of over thirty-six years revealed he could no longer continue to live as a man but had to pursue his true identity as a woman. This eventually led him to undergo sex re-assignment surgery, which today is referred to as gender-affirming surgery. I could not remain in the relationship because I understood God's design for marriage was between a woman and a man — something he no longer wished to be. So, we divorced. As a result, my world and that of our family was turned on end. I found myself reexamining our past, as well as my future and even trying to sort out what my present would look like going forward. *Mary Lee*

Past – Future – Present

The present, Dear Lord, in the present –
THIS is the place where I reside.
No longer can I live in the past.
In the future I cannot hide.

In the *PAST* I faced many sorrows,
things I so much wished I could flee.
I dare not let myself linger there
for more heartaches would come to me.

In dreams of my uncharted *FUTURE,*
I see there what I *want* to see,
but I know that's only make-believe.
Real life is here waiting for me.

Keep me focused now on the *PRESENT* –
doing that for which I'm designed.
In this, may I learn to be content
with joys You intend me to find.

Though dreaming may not be a real sin,
I must live in reality.
Help me to seek Your glory each day,
and be who You wish me to be.

In my neighborhood, this beautiful statue sits on a front lawn near the street. On the day I discovered it, I stopped and snapped this picture. Upon arriving at home, I felt lead to compose a poem —the one you see to the left. I later even made a card on which I included the photo with my poem. To me, both spoke of enduring love, and hence, the title "Love Frozen in Time". *Mary Lee*

Love Frozen in Time

They vowed how their love was forever
when they both were so fresh and young.
Sometimes for her he'd write poetry,
and on some occasions, he sung.

Admiringly, she'd gaze up at him
with eyes that would sparkle and shine.
"I am the luckiest girl" she'd say
"because, my dear husband, you're mine!"

The small bench that sat out on their lawn
was their favorite place to sit.
He'd read aloud, she'd pet her cat.
How perfectly all of them fit!

A statue of them one day was cast
It showed them in their special place.
Peace and contentment passersby saw
reflected in each wrinkled face.

As the years sped by for both of them,
their love remained constant and sure.
Their statue proclaims to all the world
how true love like theirs can endure.

When an unexpected divorce occurs, one's world is turned upside down no matter the specific cause or who was to blame. There will be pain to process, unforeseen challenges to face, and new situations with which to become accustomed. Having a compassionate friend to come along side us in these times is definitely a blessing — one I believe is often orchestrated by God Himself. Knowing how good it is to <u>have</u> a friend during difficult times, I would remind readers how good it is when we can <u>BE</u> such a friend to another who is going through trials. Just think, when we do it's like we're "the arms of Jesus" holding our friend! How great is that?   *Mary Lee*

Hole in My Heart

There is a hole, a hole in my heart
that is big and gaping and raw.
A man passed me in the grocery.
How is it that he never saw?

There is a hole, a hole in my heart.
It's so huge they'll all surely see.
How is it people I've known for years
look away as they approach me?

There's a hole, a hole in my heart
as dreams for my life slip away.
I think some friends are touched by my pain,
but they just don't know what to say.

There is a hole, that's *still* in my heart,
but *some* hope I'm starting to feel.
Friends are helping the hole start close.
Perhaps there's a chance I will heal.

Now there's a scar that covers the hole.
As time passes, God helps me see.
Friends who held me and sat by my side
in fact, were *His* arms holding me.

When I see people who are in pain,
on my heart may I feel a tug.
As I recall God's love shown to me,
I'll reach out and offer a hug.

Since I've known great pain, I understand
one's desperate need for relief.
May I commit to sit, walk, or stand
by them as they go through *their* grief.

Whatever caused a hole in *your* heart,
I know God can make it like new.
He did it for me so long ago,
and He'll also do it for you.

Even marriages that look very good on the outside may not be as healthy and happy as they appear. In 2007 when this poem was written, very few people were choosing to undergo what was then referred to as a sex reassignment surgery. In fact, most people had never even heard of such a thing. Yet, my husband of thirty-four years felt compelled to pursue what he understood to be his true female identity. It was not a decision he made lightly, and the impact on him and on our family was great. I cannot speak to its effect on others, but this poem shines light on some of the ways it initially began to impact me. *Mary Lee*

The Dilemma:
Which Box to Check

If I had the wisdom of Solomon
then I'd certainly know what to do.
I would weigh the options, decide my course,
and feel sure of what I should pursue.

All scenarios, I would consider –
how they'd impact each person involved.
I'd then proceed in the way I thought best.
The dilemma by that be would solved.

But Solomon's wisdom I don't possess,
and it's so hard to know what is right.
I feel conflicted about what to do,
and I'm restless throughout the long night.

Now the man to whom I was once married
all too quickly has faded from view.
As the 'female' self replaces the 'male',
There is nothing more I know to do.

MARITAL STATUS
[Check box]
☐ Single
☐ Married
☐ Widowed
☐ Divorced
☐ Other

He says in his heart he always has known
how inside he was not a true man.
Biology forced him to live a lie,
but he says that he no longer can.

To live as a 'she' would bring inner peace
which was never felt living as 'he',
and though this brought anguish and others' pain,
so this change he felt just had to be.

He firmly believes God will stay with him,
since God loves the true person inside.
He's also convinced the woman within
should be free and no longer denied.

It's now *my* id*entity* that's confused
when I must choose the right little square.
Am I *married*, or *single* or *widowed*?
When I come to such boxes, I stare.

While I do no feel I am a widow,
I cannot be a wife to a 'she'.
In a way, I don't feel like a single,
So, I question, "What does this make me?"

I will ask God, by His Holy Spirit,
"Give me wisdom to know what to do,"
for I'm struggling now with this dilemma,
and I so need sound guidance from You.

FAMILY ISSUES THROUGH THE SEASONS:
Parents - Children - Elderly Parents - Dementia

When a couple has a baby, they need and often receive all kinds of things as gifts. For some special couples I would write and frame a poem for the baby's nursery, often using decorative paper to match the motif they'd chosen to decorate it in. A few poems I wrote like the following one, using the *"voice"* of the baby speaking to its parents. This one was for a couple I knew in Memphis over thirty years ago. *Mary Lee*

Mommy, Daddy, and Me

It took me a long time to get here.
For weeks Mommy stayed in the bed,
but during the time they were waiting,
I heard everything that they said.

They asked God to let me be healthy.
Good parents they promised to be.
They said they both always would love me
and take really good care of me.

I like looking up at my Mommy,
whose face is so pretty and sweet.
and even though Daddy wears glasses,
I think he's both handsome and neat!

I'm proud to have Mommy and Daddy
who take me with them everywhere,
and they do not seem to mind a bit
that I don't have very much hair!

I certainly am a lucky girl
for good parents God's given me.
Together we'll have wonderful times.
The future, I can't wait to see!

Love, Your Baby Girl

No Greater Love

No one can fathom the depth of love
that can span through eternity?
It alone is the essence of God,
and it's given for all to see.

A picture of this dear, holy love
is seen in a mother with child.
Cuddling her baby close to her braest,
the scene is both tender and mild.

No matter the days and years that pass,
a mother's love stays ever strong,
and she will stand and support her child
in spite of when he has done wrong.

A mother's love will never run out
though sometimes it isn't returned.
There's nothing more god-like on earth
than love which is purely unearned.

As we observe a mother with child,
may we stop and to God give praise.
Let this reflection of God's own *love*
remain with us throughout our days.

The original version of this poem was inspired by Peggy VanBuren's pastel abstract entitled "No Greater Love." Her painting suggested Mary and the Christ child. As I reflected on what she created, I thought of the depth of love most mothers feel as they hold their babies in their arms. So, I share this poem honoring Peggy and all mothers, including my daughter-in-law, Chrissy, pictured with her three babies — Noah, Coleman, and Ian. *Mary Lee*

Do you recall how you felt about being given advice when you were young? Your parents may have been wise, but you thought you knew as much or more than they did. When you became an adult, and especially when you became a parent, your appreciation for their wisdom likely increased tremendously. In this poem, a grown child with children of their own, voices appreciation to their dad. They even eat a bit of "humble pie" acknowledging how they've found themselves telling their own children what dear, old dad had told them long ago. Ah, a ***Déjà vu*** moment! *Mary Lee*

A Dear Dad *Déjà vu* Moment

When I was young, you used to say,
"Oh boy, how the time does fly!"
Now since I have gotten older,
I know this not a lie!

You possessed a wealth of wisdom
you tried to pass on to me,
but sometimes I wouldn't listen.
It's value, I failed to see.

You gave advice meant to help me,
but I didn't want to hear.
Sometimes I did the opposite!
My life I wanted to steer.

Fast-forward, I'm now repeating
to ***my kids*** once in a while,
the very same things *you* told *me*.
(Dad, I'll bet that makes you smile!)

I never dreamed *I* would say them,
but I learned how they were true.
When my ***grandkids*** one day hear them,
then I will just smile like you!

Parent-child relationships can be challenging. This can be particularly so for mothers and daughters. When that sweet little bundle in pink begins to grow up and seems to be full of sass and vinegar, what's a mother to do? My personal childrearing experience comes from raising a son, but perhaps you'll still find something of help in this poem as a mother looks for answers and healing of the relationship between her teenage daughter and herself. *Mary Lee*

Mother and Daughter and Difficult Days

When you asked God for a blessing,
He sent this dear child to you.
He said, "I love you very much,
and I love your daughter, too."

"While it was you who carried her,
I placed her there in your womb.
It always was my plan for her
that in your heart there'd be room."

You watched in awe, as day by day
you saw your dear daughter grow.
The early years were so much fun,
you thought more of it you'd know.

Now you and she only argue
about things she cannot do.
The friction and frustrating days
destroys the joy in both of you.

You pray to have wisdom and grace,
for calmness, mercy and peace.
If these can live in both of you
then anger you can release.

Raising girls can be challenging,
but it's so worth hanging on,
for one day you'll both laugh again
once difficult days are gone.

This poem was for parents to share with their prodigal child who was now trying to make some positive changes. He knew he needed a course correction in his life, but he had experienced some starts and stops before as he tried to make changes. He had once believed in God, but other things gained his attention and allegiance. Now, he was trying to find his way back home, but it was precarious and difficult. He needed a good dose of encouragement and love from his family, and most of all, he needed to know he was still loved by God.   *Mary Lee*

Hang In There

Some days you sail as if on glass.
Some days you will hit a wall.
Some days it's hard to just get up,
and face this old world at all.

But there's no one's life that's perfect.
We each have our flaws and faults.
While traveling through this old world
we'll each have our starts and halts.

We're happy you're making progress.
We've prayed to see this in you.
If you'll keep trusting in the Lord,
so many good things you'll do.

A setback does not spell failure,
as you've made this brand-new start!
By doing this, it says a lot
about both you and your heart.

Remember, that we still love you.
We know that you can succeed!
May these words bring encouragement
for that's something we all need!.

Letting our young ones try their wings is hard, especially if it involves their moving away. But when you've done your best to prepare them, you must let them go. They know the way home, and you can remind them they'll always be welcomed should they one day need a soft place to land for a while! Affirm your faith in them as they make their new start, but don't hold on when it's time to **cut those apron strings!**

Mary Lee

Apron Strings and Young One's Wings

Don't clip wings, clip apron strings,
and let your young one soar.
Her life she has before her,
and much she has in store.

It's true there will be sorrows.
She'll have her share of pains,
but think of the joy she'll find
as confidence she gains.

You've taught her many lessons
so she will know what's right.
You've picked her up, dried her tears,
and cried with her at night.

It's now time she learns to stand
and face life on her own.
To you, she still is a child,
but *she* thinks she is grown.

Recall when you were her age,
so much you didn't know.
When your freedom you desired
your parents let you go.

Your daughter's at the crossroads.
Have faith that she'll succeed.
She knows you'll be there for her
if help, she one day needs.

Only clip your apron strings,
though it will pain your heart.
She must make her own way now.
Letting go is your part!

Know God will be there for her.
He'll help you through this, too.
It's not easy for parents,
but this we have to do.

Sometimes an adult child may still be living at home but refusing to comply with the family's rules. Their lifestyle may have become dangerous, destructive, or possibly illegal. What can parents do? This describes how one couple addressed the situation. It wasn't easy, but they felt they had tried everything else, and nothing had worked. Thankfully, they saw a happy ending, though this isn't always the outcome. These parents survived by praying often; by leaning on each other and on trusted Christian friends; and by trusting in the grace of God. Their son eventually did make necessary changes and became a productive adult who made them proud. *Mary Lee*

It's Time

How many times shall we forgive?
Once more should we open our door?
We know you need a helping hand,
and that is what parents are for.

But there's a time to close the door -
the one to our home - not our heart.
You must learn to stand on your own,
and it's time, son, you make a start.

It hurts our heats to see you crawl
for we want much better for you.
How to stand up, you must now learn
or crawling is all you will do.

Strength to one's muscles builds slowly,
each one of us starts on our knees.
First, we crawl - then toddle and fall -
'til finally, we'll walk with ease.

What kind of a loving parent
would ever want for their child to stay
crawling about as an infant –
not learning to run or to play?

It hurts to see you stumbling.
but we can't make choices for you.
So, we'll let you have your freedom
to do what you think you must do.

Dear son, know how much we love you.
We'll be praying for you each day.
But now you must stand on your own,
and your time to start is today!

The Corner

There's a little corner of my heart that's been reserved for **you**, and that tiny part you'll always own — no matter what you do.

Though
miles and years
may come between
still that corner
you may claim,
and I hope somewhere
within your heart
there's a corner with
my name.

Mom

Simple, little poems can sometimes say more than those packed with many words. The one above I first gave to my only son, Caleb, many years ago. The sentiments are as true today as they were all those years ago, and I hope they still mean as much to him as they do to me. One picture below shows me covering the top of his shaved head with some of my white hair! Seeing this always makes me smile.

Mary Lee

My precious mother,
Helen Brock

DEALING WITH DEMENTIA

While not all families will have to deal with a loved being lost in the dread disease dementia, many will. Whether it is of the Alzheimer's type or some other form, it is a long, difficult ordeal for the person afflicted and for their caregiving family.

Most of us know people who are caring for mates or elderly parents with the disease, and some of our friends have perhaps begun to exhibit some of the early signs themselves. The following four versions of a special poem were written to encourage these families. with afflicted loved ones.

The words I wrote were a result of my studies on aging, my work as a marketer for a geriatric psych unit, personal experiences with my mother, and from insights God provided to me.

My desire is that we will all be quick to show kindness and compassion to those in these situations, being mindful we may one day join their ranks. May God bless us one and all.

Mary Lee

Loving the Father Before Me

Oh God, my father is changing,
right before my eyes.
The changes are hard on each of us,
so, Lord, please help me be wise.

I loved the man I called Daddy.
He was funny, wise, and bright,
but this isn't the same man before me
who has started to wander at night..

He was robbed of strength and abilities,
and frustration can make him get mean.
The man who was once kind and happy,
around here is no longer seen.

Dear God, help me live in the present,
and love him for who he is now,
for _now_ is when he so needs me.
Dear Lord, will You please show me how.

In Jesus' Name, Amen

Loving the Mother Before Me

Oh God, my mother is changing,
right before my eyes.
The changes are hard on each of us,
so, Lord, please help me be wise.

I loved my dear precious mother.
She was kind, lots of fun, and smart,
but this isn't the woman before me
whose harsh words rip open my heart.

She was robbed of her sweet, gentle spirit,
and now she resents all I do.
Though my actions are meant to help her,
what I tell her just doesn't get through.

Dear God, help me live in the present,
and love her for who she is now,
for *<u>now</u>* is when she so needs me.
Dear Lord, will You please show me how.

In Jesus' Name, Amen

Loving the Husband Before Me

Oh God, my husband is changing,
right before my eyes.
The changes are hard on each of us,
so, Lord, please help me be wise.

I loved the man I married.
He was caring, exciting, and wise –
but this isn't the same man before me
with a lost, confused look in his eyes.

He was robbed of strength and patience
by this illness, so ugly and vile,
and the man I once loved and laughed with
has not been here for a while.

Dear God, help me live in the present,
and love him for who he is now,
for _**now**_ is when he so needs me.
Dear Lord, will You please show me how.

In Jesus' Name, Amen

Loving the Wife Before Me

Oh God, my wife is changing,
right before my eyes.
The changes are hard on each of us,
so, Lord, please help me be wise.

I loved the woman I married.
She was gentle, loving, and bright.
In the daytime she looks more lost,
then she roams the house each night.

She's missing her kind, sweet spirit,
and untrusting of things I do.
She's resentful and accusing,
so unlike the woman I knew.

Dear God, help me live in the present,
and love her for who she is now,
for <u>*now*</u> is when she so needs.
Dear Lord, will You please show me how.

In Jesus' Name, Amen

Alzheimer's in all its various forms is a horrible disease. It's been called "The Long Goodbye". Many times it is just that. In some cases, the disease slowly progresses and lingers so long the caregivers become worn down and may even pass before the afflicted person! In the later stages of the disease, individuals may (1) lose their ability to communicate, (2) may not recognize their loved ones, and (3) some may become combative and unmanageable. This poem was written for a sister in Christ, Bonita Fields, as I observed her struggling to care for her husband, Talmadge, in their home. If you are in this situation, may it encourage you.

Mary Lee

When Burdens Are Heavy

I see how stressful your days are,
and you're so much in need of rest.
With caregiving tasks you're burdened,
yet you're trying to do your best,

You witness your husband changing,
losing skills, he once did with ease.
It's heartbreaking now to see it,
especially as he tries to please.

It pains you he isn't himself,
and sometimes it's frightens, too.
Though he'd never mean to hurt you,
it's something he's liable to do.

CAREGIVING Responsibilities

What's ahead is so unwanted.
You wish this would all disappear.
It's hard living with these problems
while knowing the worst isn't here.

Don't let all this stress defeat you,
for one person can't do it all.
Please, allow your friends to help you.
All you need to do is to call.

But most of all, call on Jesus.
Believe and then follow His lead,
He'll help you care for your husband,
and supply the wisdom you need.

Occasionally, a person will develop dementia in midlife. If he or she is single, without children, and have parents who are either aged or deceased, the question arises, "Who will ensure the afflicted person is properly cared for?" If there are siblings, the responsibility may fall to them. Yet, not all are so fortunate as to have a caring family. In those instances the individual may end up being alone and homeless. In this poem siblings struggled to determine what was best for their sister and made the decisions they thought best. Still, so very sad. *Mary Lee*

What's to be Done with Sister?

Some teased calling her "Crazy Sister"
because of what she'd say and do.
In spite of poor judgment and antics,
they loved her, and this she still knew.

At first, they dismissed her behaviors.
Many choices she made were bad.
Family didn't like who she hung with,
and this made them angry and sad.

An accident damaged her body,
and her mental state soon declined.
She couldn't made sound decisions
and thought she was losing her mind.

Soon she stopped engaging with others.
She didn't know how to relate.
The same questions she would keep asking,
and she'd often forget the date.

She was scared and she felt quite alone.
It was clear, peace she did not know.
In her eyes, we would see confusion.
We wrestled with where she should go.

When she could not take care of herself
or call out for help on a phone,
the siblings stepped in and took control
for Sister could not live alone.

She seemed too young for a *"special home,"*
but better care they couldn't give.
It wasn't perfect, but she was safe,
so, that was where she went to live.

They had done their best to sort things out.
They hoped they had made the right call.
They believed this was her best option,
and also the best for them all.

Before long, their Sister passed away.
She recognized no one by then.
Her family prayed that peace she'd found
when her sad, troubled life did end.

As year after year keeps passing by
the mem'ry of Sister remains.
They dwell on the good times, not the bad,
for the Real Sister these contain.

> As we grow closer to our *expiration date*, we humans are faced with the reality of having all this **stuff** to be taken care of. In generations past, people seemed to have a greater appreciation for family heirlooms they'd had for generations. Not so these days. Thus, the old lady in this piece addresses the matter and concludes with a poignant question.
> *Mary Lee*

An Old Lady's Final Question

Many years now lay behind her –
far less of them lie ahead.
Her children now live far away.
and lots of her friends are dead

All the treasures she collected -
acquired over many years -
are now considered only "things"
on which lots of dust appears.

She has more space than she requires.
no need for it does exist.
The children's rooms are vacant.
How dearly each child is missed!

She asks, "Who'll take my nice sofa
or great-grandma's huge buffet?"
"We don't have any room for them,"
each one of the children say.

There are boxes of old photos
that ought to be handed down,
as well as some treasured linens,
though some of them have turned brown.

There's mother's old, worn out Bible
she read from for many years.
Yes, it's marked up, stained, and tattered
from use and her precious tears.

Such things today aren't important,
she sadly has come to see.
She poses one final question:
"Now what's to be done with me?"

Artist unknown

The decision described here is all too common and is one that's never easy to make. Children realize their parents won't stay self-sufficient and strong all their lives, and as they age, they will likely need help. When one of your parents can no longer do for himself or herself, and the other parent is not physically able to take up the slack, hard decisions must be addressed. This poem is about such a time. The photo is of Betty Williams and son, Terry, when she was living in a care home during Covid. Lorie Williams captured their happy visit through the glass door that day.   *Mary Lee*

A Hard Decision: Placing Mom in a Care Home

Our former roles have been reversed.
The parent I've had to become.
I've dreaded what this change would mean,
but I knew the moment would come.

I feel such pain and sadness, too,
as my white-haired mother I see.
She once dared for dad and herself.
Now she's lost that ability.

Her mind now-a-days is foggy,
and her physical health is poor.
Dad's been caring for her at home,
but now she requires so much more.

Today we signed some documents –
such a simple task one would say –
but understanding what this meant,
has made it a heart-wrenching day.

Now mom's in a new environment,
a new place where she'll now live.
We prayed it would be good for her
though we knew it would make her sad.

We struggled with the decision.
For mom and dad was this the best?
Though he was alone in their home,
at night he could finally rest.

If my kids face this dilemma,
I pray I will not give them grief.
May I with grace accept changes
designed so we'll all feel relief.

I ask them to not forget me.
Come visit me once in a while.
Fill me in on family news,
so on my face you'll see a smile.

According to God's plan for families, parents were to provide for their children's physical, educational, emotional, and spiritual needs. Mothers were typically the chief nurturers, especially of the very young. Yet in reality, children need nurturing from BOTH parents. Somewhere along the way many fathers missed out on learning to do this as they busied themselves with work and financially providing for the family. Because many men (especially those of decades past) often did not learn to connect on an emotional level with their children, these kids (especially the boys) may have failed to develop much love and respect for their fathers. Without this connection, sons often grew up to feel little responsibility toward their fathers as their dads grew older and needed help. This poem speaks to the internal struggles of one son whose father developed dementia and now needed his son's help.

Mary Lee

A Son's Prayer

Dear God, lately, dad has changed so much,
and I want to do what is right.
He wasn't the father I wanted,
and I'm wrestling with this tonight.

He provided in ways, financial.
Things I needed, I always had.
He was generous with his earnings,
making all of his friends of his quite glad.

Emotionally, he was absent,
and this bred resentment in me.
He seemed to only live for himself -
not for my mom, my sister, or me.

My dear mother now isn't living.
She never saw his muddled state.
He's now old, without work or purpose,
and to this he cannot relate.

Dementia is fast coming on him,
as he makes debts, he cannot pay.
He still believes he should be in charge,
and control he won't give away.

Soon all will come crashing in on him,
since advice he simply won't heed.
I resent him for *who he wasn't*,
yet, *now* I see dad is in need.

I know I must honor my father.
In God's Word, I've read the command.
Lord, help me to do what is needed,
though my dad will not understand.

May I also teach my own children
how hard choices we sometimes must make.
We act in the way we know is right,
and we do it for Jesus's sake.

Lord, I close by asking for wisdom,
and help so that I can forgive.
I want to show kindness to my dad
in these last years that he'll get to live.

> *When my mother had her 80th birthday she was residing in a nursing home due to increasing challenges caused by dementia. Although I was working, I was able to visit her almost every day. It wasn't a perfect situation, nor was it where she wished to be, but I felt most of the staff there cared and did their best. I wrote this piece for them with a dual purpose: (1) to recognize and applaud the staff who were caring and kind, and (2) to hopefully encourage others who were **not** as caring and kind by helping them realize how important their jobs were to the residents in their care and, by extension, to their families.*
>
> *Mary Lee*

I Am Thankful

When days are long and confusion fogs her thinking,
when she responds with agitation —
you are there to reaffirm she is safe and okay,
and I am thankful.

When she is lonely, lost and feeling out of place —
you are there to calmly talk to her, to listen to her,
and to give her a hug as you reassure her that
she isn't alone,
and I am thankful.

When she awakens in the night with a need
to wander or pace because there is *something she needs to do* or *somewhere she needs to go*,
but she can't quite remember *what* it is, or *where* it is, or *how* to get there,
you are there to help redirect and calm her,
and I am thankful.

In your relationship with her, there is no baggage,
no past misunderstandings, no unresolved anger.
There is just an opportunity to show kindness
and compassion to someone in need.
You do,
and I am thankful.

Though money is a valued commodity in the
materialistic world in which we live,
no amount of money would be enough to say
'thank you' for all you do.
Today I offer you these words instead of money
realizing they can't buy groceries or pay bills.
I hope you'll recognize they aref my way to convey
gratitude for what you do for my mother,
*and for all the mothers and fathers
for whom you provide the daily care.*

So, I close with two more "I am thankfuls":

Friends, I am thankful **TO** you,
and I am thankful **FOR** you!

May God bless each of you.

PERSONAL STRUGGLES:
Illnesses - Injuries – Depression - Addiction

> *Sometimes we find ourselves in frightening situations or circumstances. We can't imagine how we will get out of them or how anything good can possibly lie beyond them. Particularly take note of the statements in bold type. Let these remind you of three important things we all must remember: (1) we are seen; (2) we are heard; and (3) the One who sees and hears us also loves us. So we can trust Him.*
> *Mary Lee*

Unsure and Afraid?

Where you are today
and where you will be tomorrow
are not unknown to God.
He sees you!

Even when you are afraid
about what is happening to you or around you,
talk to Him about your concerns.
Believe He has a plan for your life.
He is orchestrating all the details
so that as they unfold, you will be safe.
He hears you!

One day soon
you will discover
all the wonderful blessings
He has prepared just for You,
and you will agree it was
worth all the struggles.
Trust Him!

Perhaps you know someone who suffers from chronic and sometimes debilitating pain. This described my friend for whom pain was a constant companion, David Aday, Major, USMC, (Ret.). Even before he retired from the Corps, he had begun to feel the effects of all those years of military service on his body. I hoped this poem would remind him how even though his pain prevented him from doing all he had once been able to do, he still had value. Since presenting it to him, I have shared the poem with scores of individuals who suffer from severe pain. All have said they were blessed by reading it. May you find someone you can bless by sharing it with them, or perhaps the **someone** whom it will bless today is you!

Mary Lee

An Unwanted Companion

Pain has become a companion.
He's always at my side.
I never find myself lonely.
From him, I cannot hide.

Often, I long for the good old days —
before he came to me.
Oh, how I'd like to feel good again —
but from him I can't be free.

Many times I've prayed he'd leave me
so my old self again I could be,
but the Lord would only remind me,
"My Grace is sufficient for thee."

At times, I <u>still</u> try to bargain,
telling God how much more I could do.
If only He'd see fit to heal me!
My petition to Him isn't new.

So many others before me
have no doubt prayed the same way,
and though we know that He loves us,
our pain is still with us today.

So, now I have a new prayer –
one that is hard to pray.
Please, help me Lord to accept this
and be useful to you anyway.

Though pain is still my companion –
going everywhere I go;
INSIDE, I have a new strength.
INSIDE, I know I'm whole!

This **tool**, my ole body, may falter,
but when God is the workman, you see,
great things He can still accomplish,
even with a worn tool like me!

Being able to work is a blessing. Just ask someone who can no longer do so because of age, infirmity, or injury. They will affirm what I've said is true. However, this poem was written to refute the notion that a person's value resides only in what they can do. May these words bring encouragement to anyone who finds themselves doubting their value because they can no longer work as they once did. *Mary Lee*

The Value of Work

Arise, and wipe the sleep from your eyes.
Do not let the day slip away.
There's much to be done while it is light.
Too soon comes the end of the day.

Consider your work a gift from God –
as tasks He's entrusted to you.
Use skills and strength to tackle them all
till each of them you get through.

We are blessed when our work is complete,
and we sleep much better at night.
We feel a sense of accomplishment
when we know we've done our work right.

One day our bodies won't move so well,
and we may then question our worth.
But God loves us for <u>who we are</u>,
not for <u>what we can do</u> on earth.

Do what you <u>can</u> as unto the Lord.
When time comes, then let your work go.
Rejoice that *your value is in Him!*
Now, isn't that so good to know?

No one is eager to open the door to pain or illness, and there's no good time for either. We simple must try to face it the best we can and realize all the ways we are blessed. Besides, we are not alone in going through pain. Even the Son of God experienced it, and He did so to provide us with the greatest gift imaginable—forgiveness of our sins! So, try to not dwell on your pains but rather on your blessings, and give God thanks for each one! *Mary Lee*

An Inconvenient Visitor

You won't get this memo or message:
"Will today be convenient for you
to let in pain or an illness?"
No, he shows up out of the blue!

When he calls, he will not be gracious
and he won't care he's putting you out.
He will demand his bidding you do.
"Pay attention to me!" he will shout.

The door you cannot close in his face
and expect him to just go away,
but to our Savior, you can call out
saying, "Lord, help me get through this day."

God's son knew both suffering and pain.
He has felt more than you're going through.
But, when you're weary, you He'll sustain,
as He lends strength and courage to you.

Now your visitor will not like this,
for his goal is to discourage you.
If he sees you listing your blessings,
He will know that your faith is quite true.

Since you follow The Great Physician,
perhaps one day He'll grant you a cure.
If not, know He'll never desert you
for His love for you ever is sure.

When a person who has always been healthy and engaged in serving others finds himself or herself out of commission and in need of help, it can be a humbling experience. They learn first-hand how being on the receiving end of help is not always easy (or sometimes easy to swallow). Consider the difficulty the Apostle Peter had when Jesus wanted to wash his feet—a task normally performed by a servant. Yes, even in such a time as when we are physically [or otherwise] in need, God can still teach us a valuable lesson like humility. May we be willing to recognize and accept such with grace and gratitude. *Mary Lee*

When A Servant Is '*Out of Commission*'

I didn't know what to do for you,
since you wouldn't say what you need.
I thought I could get you a good book,
but I heard you don't like to read.

I thought I might bring you some flowers,
or some art to put on your wall,
or maybe a rack for your neat hats
that you could hang up in your hall.

But what could I give to cheer you up,
when you're down and you need a hand -
when you've had to admit you need help,
and for that you never had planned.

I know all of this isn't easy -
to let others look after you.
You may refuse service like Peter,
since serving is something <u>you</u> do.

In this down time look for the lesson
that for you God might have in mind.
Let others now minister to you,
and thank them for being so kind.

Dear friend, may you soon feel much better.
May your health be restored to you.
Consider that your gift to others
is what you allow **them** to do!

Any of these books by friends — most from Arkansas — could certain cheer one who is ill.

Shortly after the suicide of the beloved actor and comedian, Robin Williams, I wrote this poem and submitted it to our local newspaper which graciously printed it. My purpose was not merely to offer a tribute to Mr. Williams but also to point out the seriousness of depression, especially when it goes undiagnosed and untreated. Just as the death of Robin Williams was a tragic loss, so too are the losses of many of our family members and friends who take this path. May God bless each of us with greater awareness, compassion, and wisdom so that we can help people struggling with depression that is perhaps so severe they consider trying this "remedy" which is no remedy at all.

Mary Lee

A Beloved Clown's Depression Battle
[*Response to the Death of Robin Williams*]

Behind all the laughter was sadness
he wore like a mask or disguise.
Through humor, he fought depression -
with the wit and jokes we did prize.

When Robin was with other people,
he would joke and make them all laugh.
Did he think people wouldn't love him
if he showed to us his other half?

A clown will disguise what is inside.
With antics, they hide how they feel.
As long as they are in the spotlight,
they'll pretend their pain isn't real.

But the weight they carry in down times,
can destroy their joy and their hope.
Too often the burdens they carry
convince them that they cannot cope.

Depression is an evil liar
distorting truth so folks believe
their life is no longer worth living,
and like him, they may choose to leave.

It's so sad they won't hear our tributes
and laments from those left behind.
Yet, praises would not have been enough
to have caused them to change their mind.

My friend, if you battle this illness,
it's not something you must conceal.
Don't let pains and hurts within your soul,
rob you of the joys you could feel.

Don't put on a false mask or makeup.
Let your true self by us be known.
Get help and keep fighting the battle,
victory o'er this you can own.

Some people think it is normal to get caught up in troubles and always expect the worst is just around the corner. I have done so myself on more than one occasion, but thinking the worst, like Winnie the Pooh's friend Eeyore, gets a person nowhere, and it only leaves them more depressed. One day I must have been enumerating my "woe is me" list when a dear friend, Pat Marek, shared something her elderly mother, Geneva Glasgow, had often repeated to her when she was down: *"Today's not tomorrow, Patricia."* There is a lot of wisdom in her words. May this little poem encourage you to look on the bright side.

Mary Lee

Today's Not Tomorrow
[Counsel from A Wise Woman]

We cannot know what tomorrow will bring,
nor whether in it, we will laugh or sing.
It is a ***present***, unopened today,
so, what we'll find in it, we cannot say.

Trust in God's love, in His mercy and grace.
Believe *anything* He can help us face.
'Today's not tomorrow,' her mother said,
so don't let the 'What If's' fill up your head.

Stop all your worry of what's yet to be.
The future we know isn't ours to see.
Just live for Jesus, and walk in His way,
and make the most of your **gift** called ***TODAY***!

There are times when someone you care for dearly is experiencing tough challenges. These may be related to physical health issues or to emotional turmoil. You may wish you could take their struggles away or in some way help to bear them. Even if you can't do either of these, there's one thing you can do for others what <u>will</u> help — ***pray!***
Mary Lee

Faith In Spite Of ...

Keep your faith in spite of sorrow.
Keep your faith in spite of pain.
Keep faith and look for the rainbow
God said would follow the rain.

There are times I'd like to hold you
tightly in my loving arms,
let you rest against my shoulder
and I'd keep you from all harms.

But in life we all face hard times,
so courage we need to find.
We must keep trusting in Jesus
with all of our heart and mind.

While I can't take this pain from you,
nor give you health back to you,
I *can* lift your name to Heaven,
and this, every day I'll do.

Just An Innocent Plant

I found an interesting plant, growing wild and free.
It looked so attractive and vibrant;
I brought a piece home with me.

I planted a tiny runner with the roses in front of my house.
It was just a sprig of green then,
and it spread like a quiet, little mouse.

Soon it grew till it covered my roses.
Then it inched right up my tree.
It ran over all the shrubs,
till no surface from it was free.

It attached itself to my home,
then my rooftop it overcame.
What once had been a pretty brick house
would never again be the same.

When I planted it in my garden,
there had never been even a doubt.
I thought if I didn't like it, I simply would pull it out.

I then believed **I controlled it**,
but eventually, **it controlled me**.
So, now I'm trapped in a prison of green,
and **Kudzu** is all I see.

~~~~~

Of course, kudzu is a plant that cannot be tamed, but "what" have you planted in your garden? What is your Kudzu's name?

Of course this poem was NOT about Kudzu but rather about addiction. While both can be fast-growing, invasive, and hard-to-eradicate, addiction can be the more sinister of the two. For the addict, the condition is ugly and generates a plethora of problems. Unfortunately, it also spawns problems and sorrows for the families of the addicts. Of course, no one starts on this journey thinking, *"I want to become addicted to _____."* Most only plan to indulge their pleasure for a little while, then they'll stop before it becomes a problem. They don't realize (or want to admit) how once their drug of choice takes control, they will sacrifice anything and anyone for a quickly fleeting high.   *Mary Lee*

> Some years ago, I was privileged to participate in the startup of a Celebrate Recovery program. There I met some good people who had been on a wrong path and wanted to get on a right one. As they were in the depths of depression or struggling with addiction, the last thing most wanted to see was their own image in a mirror. However, as they worked their program, some found hope and the ability to smile at their "new" image in the mirror as a result of finding Jesus and getting clean.
>
> *Mary Lee*

The *New* You in Your Mirror

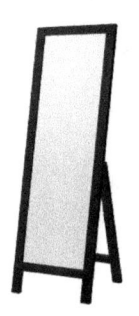

I've prayed for you so often.
In fact, I did it today!
I prayed that God would help you,
so you would soon find your way.

I've prayed peace God would give you -
to dwell down, deep in your heart,
so, you'd feel calm and secure
as you make this brand new start.

Soon, looking in your mirror,
you'll find a smile on your face –
one depression and sadness
won't have the power to erase.

The new you in that mirror
all of us will get to see,
as hope you found in Jesus
helps you live happy and free.

No one wants to be considered a loser on life's scoreboard. Yet, no one can win all the time. Often the most successful people in business and in life will speak of some failure they once encountered that spurred them on to later success. Spiritually speaking, the Apostle Paul wrote about being strong when he was weak. He discovered his true strength was found in Jesus, not in himself. So, consider carefully your "losses". Perhaps the lessons you gain from them will turn out to be some of life's best blessings to you *OR TO OTHERS!* *Mary Lee*

Reframing A Loss

When you have had a loss or defeat
so if fairness in life you doubt,
do you think of others you can blame,
or do you try thinking it out?

When you gave all to a certain task,
yet the outcome seemed so unfair.
When someone else was given the prize,
did you sink down in your despair?

Why weren't you the one called the winner?
That title you surely deserved.
When others enjoyed the winner's feast,
defeat was the dish you were served.

Could something worthwhile be learned from this
that only could come through a loss?
If so, it must be quite valuable
since it came with such a high cost.

Think very hard about what transpired.
What lesson were you meant to learn?
Don't let frustration, anger, and pain
be the only *trophies* you earn.

Instead, recognize even in loss
there's a way that you can succeed
If Christ-like behavior you display
that may be what other folks need.

Perhaps, no scoreboard reflects **that** win
if in Christ, it is a new brother
who witnessed in you the kind of life
they've been longing to discover!

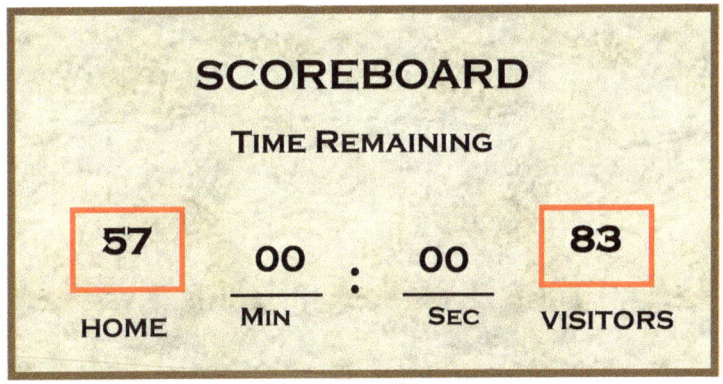

> Even doctors get sick and sometimes need surgery! Silly statement, but nevertheless true. This was written in the '90's for Dr. Tony Hooker, a dentist, who was the first person I knew to have open heart surgery. He came through the procedure well, but there were some anxious moments leading up to and after the surgery for him and his young wife. With this poem I wanted to remind him of God's part in his 'salvation' – both the first time and **this time**! I also hoped it would encourage him to consider how _he was saved to serve and save_!
> *Mary Lee*

A Second Salvation

While resting up from your surgery,
there must be so much on your mind.
Perhaps gratitude overwhelms you
as you ponder God who's so kind.

It's truly a wonderful marvel –
the things that the doctors can do,
but the One who controls the outcome.
is *God* who is now healing you!

Each day as your body gets stronger,
I'll pray for your spirit to thrive,
A wonderful purpose God must have had
for which He has kept you alive.

Delight in the joy of salvation.
A *second salvation* you've known!
With gratitude, now share your story,
since mercy to you He has shown.

Roadblocks and challenges come to all of us as we make our way through life. For individuals dealing with the prospect of getting and staying clean and sober, these challenges can be daunting. May the words of this poem be helpful to anyone seeking to encourage another in their journey toward (or continuous in) sobriety. *Mary Lee*

Roadblocks Can't Stop Blessings

While on your recovery journey,
a difficult path it will be.
You will face a number of roadblocks,
as your true self, you come to see.

It is like when a mountain climber
says this one is too high to scale.
The problem is *not* the mountain's height.
Not Trying to Climb makes him fail.

Continue to push yourself forward,
and count upon God to assist.
In the end, you can find victory
and *success* you won't have to miss.

By pressing on, you will get stronger –
in body, in mind, and in heart.
God's Spirit will also strengthen you.
Trust Him, for He will do His part.

If a friend in danger is walking,
what advice to him can you give?
Will you tell him, "Do not stop trying.
Find joy in a new way to live."

Say truthfully, "It won't be easy,
but with God, you'll make it each day."
Then add, "I'm a work still in progress,
but this is a much better way."

Go out now and share your own story.
Perhaps others' courage will grow.
As they see how God has blessed your life,
a new life they may come to know.

> We rejoice when someone "rings that bell" declaring their treatments are over and they have been declared "cancer free". Such was the case with a dear sister in Christ from Memphis, Ernestine Miller. However, sometimes cancer will return as it did for her. This poem was written to encourage her to keep on fighting while realizing the battle belongs to God. He will stay with us all the way — even if we have to go into battle a second time! *Mary Lee*

In Times Like These
[When the "Big C" Has Returned]

It's true, I don't know the direction
or way God would have me choose.
My enemy has returned again,
and this time I fear could lose.

I admit that the future scares me,
and I worry about the pain.
Should we fight this thing aggressively?
If so, what may I hope to gain?

I need so much to feel God's presence,
though I know that He's here with me.
The doubts and fears at times like these
can blind me so it's hard to see.

Fighting The Big "C" Again

Dear God, may I always keep trusting
that You'll remain close by my side.
No matter if it gets really bad,
remind me, with me you'll abide?

This battle is just temporary,
and it will *not* decide the war.
So, whatever may be the outcome,
for me you have good things in store.

I'm thankful to you, dearest Father.
You love me and wish no harms.
I ask You to now draw me closer
in Your tender, protective arms!

> Doubts and fears can attack any of us, especially when we have received a diagnosis suggesting our illness may be terminal. This essay addresses some of the challenges and anxieties a person in this situation can face. May it serve as a reminder that in ALL THINGS our best course of action includes trusting in God—something that requires faith in His power, His promises, and His great love. May these thoughts bless all who may be in such a situation. *Mary Lee*

Diagnosis, Doubts, Fears, and Grace

This diagnosis has me so messed up and frightened, and I'm really struggling. Sometimes it's hard to remember God knows exactly what I'm facing. He cares how I hurt, and *how much I fear hurting more* – perhaps **much more**. I'm concerned about my loved ones and friends. As a Christian, I question whether I did all I could to help them and others to know Jesus and learn to trust Him? And now – do *I* trust Him when it's a "rubber meets the road" situation? I really *want* to, but fears, as well as pain, are major obstacles. I've found no single answer to calm me. At times, it's nearly impossible to pray. How can I make it?

I guess I'm like the Apostle Paul — wanting God to take all this from me. Paul repeatedly prayed for God to take his physical "thorn" away, but God didn't. Instead, He told him, "My grace is sufficient." I ask myself, "What does *grace* have to do with my situation – with what I am going through now or with what I'm worrying about?'

Hum. **Worrying About.** Yes, I admit I'm worrying. I know

worry is an outgrowth of fear, and fear comes from a lack of faith. Maybe God is trying to get me to understand how He doesn't want me to worry, but instead He wants me to believe He will take care of me. I **want** to, but right now, I'm not completely there. My faith feels very small. Yet, if I have this right, God understands this. In His **grace** He's telling me, "I've got this! You won't have to go through it alone."

Yes, God loves me even when I'm struggling, hurting, and angry because I'm not better and may not get better. He's still with me even when my emotions make it impossible for me to voice my prayers. This must be one of those times when grace comes in. I must remember all the anxiety I am experiencing and the doubts assailing me **do not** separate me from God because His grace covers these and me. His Spirit intercedes for me in times when I'm weak – *like now*. He reminds me I am loved no matter what! I can trust He will **always** uphold me in His mighty, loving arms.

So, maybe it is finally starting to sink in. Whether I regain my health here or whether I re-locate earlier than I had anticipated to the perfect heavenly home Jesus has prepared for me, it is okay. I have **faith** I will be all right because God is good, and He loves me! I can do this! Thank you, Father, for this much-needed reminder.

> Sometimes people observe a Christian experiencing difficult health issues, and they may question, "Where is his or her God at a time like this?" It always encouraged me when I've witnessed Christians like Pat McRee, a dear sister from Memphis, who continued to trust God through countless cancer battles and surgeries. In doing so, she demonstrated not only her faith but also her faithfulness. While this was initially written with Pat in mind, it became something perfect for sharing with others who faithfully endured so much, and yet they continued to trust and praise God!   *Mary Lee*

Where Is Your God?
[*A Powerful Testimony*]

When people see me looking tired, sad,
or a bit forlorn because of the challenges I am facing,
they may wonder,
"Where is your God in times like these?"
They may believe He has forgotten me,
or that my prayers are unheard,
but they are mistaken.

My God has been with me the entire journey —
from diagnosis to treatments,
and He will remain with me
through successes or setbacks.

My God, hovers close to my bedside,
sits with me in the waiting rooms,
and is even there when buckets are held for me,
and my forehead is being wiped.

My God sent me doctors and hospital personnel
who minister with His kindness and care.
He continually hugs my family and me
with the loving arms of friends
who know our struggles.
He encourages us with uncountable cards,
texts, calls, and visits coming at the precise moments
when they are most needed.

So, when anyone asks,
'Where is your God?'
I tell them:
My God is where He has always been,
every moment of the long days and the longer nights.
Even when the challenges
might try to convince me I am alone.
I choose to praise and thank Him for loving me and
for always being right here with me!

> Facing a life-threatening illness like cancer can cause a person to experience life differently than before. For some, their daily focus may shift and their perspective may become distorted. They may come to view the world through the "lens" of their disease. Others may choose not to allow their illness to determine how they see life and their approach to the future. This essay was written for and inspired by a friend, Annette Stokes, as she chose to face her cancer like the person depicted in Scenario Three. *Mary Lee*

Three Approaches to A Life-Threatening Illness

Scenario One: *Depressed and Hopeless*

When she awoke it was a bright, sunny day – beautiful in fact. She looked outside and asked herself, "Even though it's nice outside, how can I feel cheery or joyful today? This cancer is continuing to attack my body, and I'm having to go through round after round of sickening treatments and terrible pain. I'll never get better."

Scenario Two: *Angry and Questioning Why*

The man glanced out the window, and all he saw was dark skies. The forecast called for storms. The depressing weather matched the darkness in his soul as he approached another day in his cancer battle. He used to believe in God, and he even went to church some, but somewhere along the way he started doubting if God even existed. Now, he was pretty sure He didn't. What kind of a god would let people suffer like he was suffering? He was bitter and wondered if he would survive. If he didn't, what might happen then?

Scenario Three: *Trusting and Assured*

She sat up in her bed after a night of little sleep. Her body ached. She was scheduled to receive chemo again today, and she knew it would be hard. Before getting out of bed, she closed her eyes and began to pray. "Dear Father, I don't know what today will bring, but I thank you for letting me awaken to see it. I will praise you if the sun is shining brightly or if rain is falling by the bucket loads. You have brought me this far, and I believe you will bring me through whatever may lie ahead. Although I want to get better and live longer, my main desire is to honor you in whatever time I am given. So please, help me shine the light of Jesus today so everyone I encounter can see Him living in me. In His precious name I pray. Amen."

People all around us are going through challenges, often quite significant ones, but many don't wish to burden others by complaining about them. As Christians, we are called to help one another, whether or not the other person even believes in Jesus. In fact, our being willing and able to help individuals who **don't** know Him may be just what is needed to draw them closer to Him! So, let us look for opportunities to show compassion and care whenever and to whomever we can.

Mary Lee

I Care and So Does God

I don't understand the reason
this trouble has now come your way.
As your friend, I feel bewildered –
not knowing just what I should say.

Of course, I can say I'm sorry,
but these words seem shallow and trite
when you face difficult issues
and wrestle with them day and night.

None of us can see the future,
or know what we'll face down the road.
We simply must do what we can,
trusting God to help with our load.

But if *I* can somehow help you,
or perhaps assist with some task,
don't think you would be imposing.
I'd feel honored if you would ask.

So, with faith, keep moving forward,
no matter how dark things appear.
God controls all our tomorrows!
Let Him help you to face each fear.

When we recognize how much like foolish sheep we are, what else should we do but listen to the call of our Good Shepherd. He not only knows us, but we are fiercely loved by Him as well. What also amazes me is I am not just a numbered beast to Him. He knows my name and He cherishes me! Now, how great is that!

Mary Lee

Your Loving Embrace

When difficult times are before me,
to no one but You can I go.
Though often I've taken my own way,
I'm grateful You still love me so.

You're my Shepherd, who's always ready
to rescue this one foolish lamb
when I've strayed into dangerous places
and forgotten **Whose** sheep I am.

Lord, help me to keep on the right path
when temptations draw me away.
Help me not get entangled or lost.
Instead, close to You help me stay.

I need much more time in your presence,
for it's there I'm blessed by Your grace.
When I finally cease my strivings,
I'll rest in your loving embrace.

END OF LIFE ISSUES:
Anticipating Death – Death - Grief

> To receive the diagnosis of a terminal illness can be earth shattering. What does one do? A natural response is to ask, "Isn't there something else we can try?" Unfortunately, sometimes there isn't, and the unknown must be faced. If this future means our death will come sooner than we had anticipated, can we as Christians **still** praise God, believing our death serves as the entrance to an eternity we will get to spend with Him? May the following thoughts help you or a friend to focus on your **true** future, and may it be one where you find peace with our Lord.
>
> *Mary Lee*

Struggling with the Prognosis

If I asked God to give me more time,
what good from more time would I gain?
Would my life be like it was before,
or would I have more time for pain?

If extra days with doctors were filled —
long hours to just sit and wait —
would these extra days be worth it all
since in death, we all find our fate?

All our days were ordained long ago
by God in His wisdom and grace.
WHEN it will end doesn't count as much
as the way that we finish our race.

Let health not be our only concern
but rather in what way we'll live.
Let us give God thanks and praise His name
for each day He chooses to give!

May His plans we seek to accomplish —
do things He's ordained us to do.
He'll give us the days we need for them
if to Him we're faithful and true.

Each day of our lives, let's do our best,
and trust Him to show us the way.
Whenever the end of our days come,
we know that it will be okay.

The Testimony of Beautiful Flowers

I love my flowers,
both inside and out.
That they've blessed my life,
I haven't a doubt.

In them God's displayed
magnificent care
with colors and shapes
He has a great flare.

He could have made earth
in greys, blacks, and whites,
but then we'd have missed
some beautiful sights.

Though it's all too soon
my flowers will fade,
I have enjoyed them
the time they stayed.

So, too with loved ones
I've been blessed to know.
Though it breaks my heart
when I see them go.

My life they enriched
because they were here,
and now in my heart,
they'll always be near.

When someone we love is nearing death or has recently passed, it may be easy to question why wouldn't God intervene and allow them to live longer. We reason how with additional years they could have blessed more people with their talents, humor, knowledge, and kindness. However, one wiser than we determines our days, both those of our birth and our death. So, let us try to focus so much on the passing of our loved one as on the blessings they brought us and others during their lifetime. For like the beautiful flowers, one day we will all pass away. *Mary Lee*

Each of us approaches our pending death differently. This poem was written for and shared with ninety-four-year-old Bill Berry shortly before his death. As a WWII veteran, Mr. Bill lived a long, colorful life. He openly acknowledged how in the first half he had been quite a rough fellow. Then in the second half, he got to know God and the forgiveness of Jesus. Bill became a changed man. He learned to love people and found much joy in serving others, especially through his volunteer work with the American Red Cross. Mr. Bill's last half was good and positive, and it brought him and others much joy. What a blessing he was to all who knew him! *Mary Lee*

As My Days Grow Fewer

Old death is crouching in the corner,
and he's waiting to pounce on me.
I know my time is growing shorter,
but I won't let him frighten me.

My body's starting to surrender.
One day from it, I'll gain release.
Constant fatigue and bonds of pain –
soon the power of these will cease.

My spirit will fly unencumbered
to the place my Lord has prepared.
Though I do not know all the details,
for my exit, I am not scared.

This is because I trust my Father
who sent Jesus to save my soul.
He took the sins and guilt I'd carried.
By His blood, I'm now pure and whole.

Old Death, come on when you are ready,
but you'll not claim a victory.
For since I gave my life to Jesus,
my home in heaven waits for me.

When a loved one's death is approaching and they need special attention and care, there is no better place for them to be than in a good facility that provides hospice care — somewhere like the Flo and Phil Jones Hospice House in Jonesboro, AR. The primary goal of hospice care is for patients to have sufficient pain management for their last days and hours and for them and families to be able to spend time with each other in a quiet, peaceful environment. The Hospice House and their caring staff have made this a reality for so many families in our region. Although this poem was written specifically with this facility in mind, other similar facilities that provide hospice care also deserve the tribute. May all of them and their staffs be blessed for the kindness they show.   *Mary Lee*

The Hospice House Experience

Your loved one has lingered through one more night,
There are no words that will make things right.
Your consolation - their pain is controlled.
Though there's little time, you have been told.

You feel so blessed by this comforting place.
You sit and study your loved one's face.
Can they understand the words that you say
as you speak to them and as you pray?

For teaching you much and loving you well,
your words of thanks to them, may you tell.
When their time is over and they have gone,
it will be so hard to carry on.

So, when 'goodbye' comes, grant them their release,
then may you all experience peace.

A Word to Caring Friends

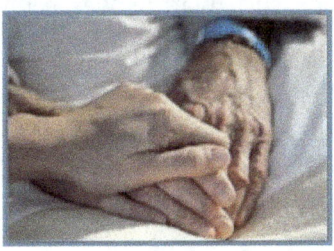

When You Don't Know What To Do

If you have a friend who's loved one is in hospice care, do not always assume they would *not* want you to visit. The hours a family spends sitting and waiting with their loved one can be long and draining. Check with the staff or with someone close to them to see if visitors are being allowed. If so, drop by for a short stay. Perhaps take them a milkshake, some fruit, a sandwich, etc. Once there, a family member will sometimes stay for many hours without eating or drinking. Furthermore, you may find that the person in care might be able to drink a Sonic Slush or eat a small ice cream. You won't know unless you ask.

Once there, generally keep your visit short. Give your friend a hug, a pat on the back, or simply provide a listening ear. It may be that the one in care can also receive a hug, but know if they can **before** you offer one. Sometimes their body or skin may be quite fragile.

If you and they are comfortable with doing so, offer to pray for the individual, their family, and/or for the people providing their care. This may be one of the best gifts you ever give.

We've all known some brave but weary warriors who have valiantly fought terminal illnesses. Seeing their strength, courage, and desire to live inspired us. One such warrior was a Christian friend, Dana Hayes, who fought cancer and then was attacked by Leukemia. She continued fighting for as long as possible. She wanted to live for her children and her grands. Her faith in God was strong and also her love for her church family. But there came a time when her body was too weak to go on, and she surrendered to rest. I penned this poem for her just days before her passing. Perhaps you know some other brave warriors it could bless.   *Mary Lee*

For A Brave but Weary Warrior

You now may be too weak to read this,
but know I am praying for you.
This battle's been especially tough
with all you've already been through.

You have been a brave, valiant warrior,
but even such warriors get tired.
Just know as you've fought so very hard,
so many of us you've inspired.

If you are too tired for this battle,
don't feel bad if you need to cease.
We've witnessed your faith and courage.
It's okay for you to seek peace.

Rest safely, as you feel God's comfort –
the kind that alone He can give.
You'll find healing here or in heaven.
We praise God that you got to live.

You've honored your Father and Jesus
as you've fought with grace and a smile.
So, even if you must now leave us now,
we know we'll see you in a while.

This painting by an unknown artist has made the rounds on Facebook. Some variations of it depict a young woman rather than the man seen here. On occasion, I have even made modifications of the picture so that it resembled an older man or woman for whose family I wished to send a special sympathy card. To me the picture portrayed the utter joy of a believer when they have finally finished their earthly race by running into the waitng arms of Jesus. What a wonderful experience to look forward to, a perfect ending to a life well-lived! *Mary Lee*

As I Near the End of My Race

With my days here on earth slipping away,
Lord, may I still find the strength to pray.
May I recognize how all isn't lost,
since You, my Savior, have paid the cost.

Although what awaits me is not quite clear,
I'm not worried, for to You, I'm dear.
You've been with me on this journey called life.
You've given me children and a dear wife.

As I'm approaching the end of my run,
I will not complain about things not done.
I have seen beauty, known friends, kind and true,
and all of these gifts I received from You.

When my race ends, help my loved ones to know
I'll be in Heaven where I pray they'll go.
I know when I get there, it will be grand,
and I can't wait to take Jesus's hand!

When a friend I called "Brother Steve" was diagnosed with advanced pancreatic cancer, he and his wife, Deb, made the hard decision not to pursue treatments. He wanted to remain in their home with her until the end came. It was an increasingly difficult period as he grew weaker. During their journey, they clung tightly to each other and to God. I wrote this poem to honor them. [After Steve passed, Deb shared how she would never recommend their approach to others. It took a terrible toll on her physically as well as mentally, and this was something Steve would NOT have wanted.] *Mary Lee*

In These Terrible Times

The circumstances we're facing,
look impossible to bear,
but we trust in Your love for us,
and we thank You for Your care.

Without You we could not make it
through one more terrible day,
but You provide us with Your peace
when we bow our heads and pray.

As we lay our needs before You,
we acknowledge Your great power.
It's only by the strength You lend,
that we've survived to this hour.

Each day we will bow and thank You
for showing to us Your love
and giving this assurance -
that we'll meet You up above.

In the winter of 1996 a dear Christian couple, Ludis and Mike Reaves, were caring for their dying, adult daughter, Rebecca, in their home. It was heartbreaking to see. I had only met her a couple of times, and this was after she was already very ill. Ludis said Rebecca liked poetry, so I was able to read some to her a couple of times before she passed. As her end drew closer, I knew people nearing death sometimes needed to be given permission to let go, so I wrote this poem for her parents to share with her. After her mom read it, she asked me if I would read it to Rebecca. I did, and all of us cried together. I was grateful I could bless them, and they blessed me, too. *Mary Lee*

It's Okay to Leave

It's okay for you to leave us.
It's okay for you to go.
It's true, that we all will miss you,
for you know we love you so.

But our God is waiting for you,
and soon angels He will send
to bring you to a resting place
where all your pain will end.

Don't worry about our sorrow.
God's comfort we will receive,
for each day He will sustain us.
This promise, we all believe.

Rest now, our precious Rebecca.
From your struggles feel release.
When you're in your heavenly home,
forever you'll be at peace.

Widowhood is a daunting experience. Spouses who have lost their mates after many years of togetherness often say things like, "It's as if a part of me is missing." This statement is a testimony to a good marriage. I wrote this poem for a Memphis friend, Bill Hall, when he lost his beloved dear wife, Joanne. Since then, it has been shared with many new widows/widowers through the years in hopes it would bless them.

Mary Lee

I Wasn't Ready

There was no way I could be prepared,
though it did not come suddenly.
Now I am left with such emptiness
since you are no longer with me.

There were things I wanted to tell you -
so much more I'd wanted to share!
But now I just sit here all alone
and silently stare at your chair.

My mind and my body feel numbness,
and it fills every inch of me.
Will someone come and awaken me?
From my nightmare, please set me free!

But I know it's real - I must face it,
though I don't know where to begin.
How can I live without my dear wife
for she was my very best friend?

What would she today have to tell me,
if once more her voice I could hear?
No doubt, she would just try to calm me,
and tell me, "Don't worry, my dear.

Our life here together was lovely.
We were blessed in so many ways.
It wouldn't be right now to question
the *quantity* of all our days."

So, this I will try to remember
as widowhood I now begin.
I'll keep looking forward to Heaven
where we'll be together again!

> Many people find it difficult to convey their sympathy and concern for someone who is grieving – especially when their grief is so great it may become debilitating. This letter is an example of something one could share with a widow, specifically if both she and her husband had loved and followed the Lord. Let it be a guide for you to use to encourage your friend as I hope it encourages my friend, Becky Allen, while reminding her of the great love our Father has for her and work she may yet have to do.
>
> *Mary Lee*

Dear Becky,

As you are trying to adjust to your new life without Ken, I know it's hard. Though it has been several weeks since he passed, it may feel like an eternity on one hand and like it was yesterday on the other.

While you may want to crawl into a hole and never come out, you know that is NOT what Ken would want for you. He loved you so much. I suspect he would want you to do your best to go on with your life – to seek a renewed purpose and eventually find renewed joy. He would also want you to remember God still has more blessings to pour into your life and more blessings for you to share with others. So, be willing to open your eyes to such things and thank God for them.

With all this in mind, dear Becky, I pray your life will eventually be less painful and more peaceful. Till then, keep trusting in God's love to provide you with strength and the will to go on – *one day at a time*. Remember, I am here for you. Many people loved Ken and all of you, and he will continue to be missed.

With Christian love,

Who can adequately describe what someone feels after the loss of their beloved mother? Mere words cannot fully convey what made her so special and why going on without her sometimes feels so crushing? In this short poem I tried to point out a couple of key things about this lady's mother and about the positive influence she had had on her daughter. *Mary Lee*

Honoring A Good Mother

On some days your grief is so heavy,
as you think of your mother, dear.
You wish once more you could talk with her,
and see her again sitting near.

Don't let yourself sink in depression,
for she would not want that for you.
Remember instead, good times you had
and the special things she would do.

Remember her smile and her sweetness.
Remember each one of her ways
for each was a part of her nature
for which we all now give her praise.

Her life truly made a difference,
and we see that she taught you well.
The influence of a good mother
on her child is easy to tell!

Though she's physically gone, she's with us,
touching lives all along the way.
Through <u>you</u>, we can still see her kindness,
and this honors her every day.

> As we seek to grow our families, sometimes things do not go as we would have desired. The couple for whom this poem was written had one precious son, but they had wanted to have more children. They were disappointed by this miscarriage and by numerous failed attempts to adopt. Although today they remain just three, theirs is a beautiful and happy family who inspires all who know them.
> *Mary Lee*

Grieving Your Unborn Child

Those who have not been through it
simply cannot understand.
Folks say, "It will get better"
as they gently pat my hand.

I know they want to show love
to both my husband and me,
but they cannot know our pain,
and our son they did not see.

As our child grew in my body,
we longed to have him here —
to look at his tiny feet
and plant kisses on each ear.

Would he have favored daddy?
Would he grow up to be tall?
Would his hair be blond like mom's?
None of this mattered at all.

Another child we'd wanted
who we could hold in our arms –
one to teach about God's love,
protecting them all harms.

Our sweet little one did not live
so our care he could receive.
Now a great sorrow we must face
as in our own ways we grieve.

There's one true thing we'll cling to,
to help us get through each night.
Our son's at home in Heaven now
with God and the angels bright.

One day we'll be with our dear son,
embracing him lovingly.
There, together in heaven
we'll be for eternity.

> SUICIDE: Whether the person who took this action was young or old; was infirmed or physically fit; was in a stupor due to drugs or alcohol; had experienced a breakup; or was suffering from depression, etc., the aftermath is terrible for those who they left behind—those who loved them. I first shared a version of this poem with a Christian couple in Memphis whose teenage daughter had taken her life. Since then, there have been far too many other families with whom it has been shared.
> *Mary Lee*

A Prayer for Understanding and Comfort

Oh how our hearts are broken!

We knew she was miserable, in pain,
    and feeling as if there was no relief in sight,
    but, we question over and over, why this had to happen.

Now it is those of us who are left behind who are miserable, in
    pain, and feeling as though there is no relief in sight for us.

We are sad, empty, lonely, and confused.
    We loved her so much.
    Others loved her, too.
    Now we must learn to live without her,
    and we don't quite know what to do or how to feel.

We realize coping with loss is never easy.
    No one is ever ready to say goodbye and sever the physical
    connection that has bound us to our loved one for so long.
    Yet, when one loses a child as we have, it seems doubly hard.

We should have had more time with our daughter,
> but she robbed us of that time.
> Maybe this is a part of why we feel so hurt
> and even angry.
> We still needed her and we wanted her with us.

Now we are left only with her memory as we offer this prayer:

Dear Father,

We call out to you in our sorrow and confusion as all of us who loved our girl go through this valley. Please hold our hands and let us feel Your presence. Take from us the hurt, the confusion, and the feelings of anger that tries to seep into our hearts so that we can properly grieve her loss.

Help us remember all the good times — the laughter and the joy we experienced with her through the years. Let these memories bring peace and comfort for our aching hearts.

Please Lord, help us to understand and go on.

In Jesus' name, we pray.
Amen.

Grief is a sickness of the heart caused by loss. It is one of the most difficult things we will ever have to deal with. There are no rules as to *HOW* one should experience it or *FOR HOW LONG* it will last. Much has been written about grief by individuals who were weighed down by it. Often, they choose poetry, *the language of the heart,* to express their sorrow or pain. The poem here was written to remind a grieving family how each of them will process grief in their own way. It points out how grieving *differently* does not mean one person's grief is less than another's. In times of loss all of us hurt. Therefore, we must strive to show compassion and kindness to one another.   *Mary Lee*

Differing Ways of Expressing Grief

People have different ways of grieving.
Some will not grieve as you do.
If some hold their grief tightly inside,
don't think they're not hurting, too.

Some cannot slow down after a loss.
They push on as they did before.
You may conclude that they didn't care,
yet they may be grieving much more.

While some of us are an open book,
and we voice all that's on our mind.
We *want* to talk, and we *need* to talk,
though listeners are hard to find.

To one another we must show grace
for the loss we all bear is great.
How long will it hold us in its grip?
Since we can't predict, we must wait.

Grief will cling very tightly to us.
It never wants to leave our mind.
Yet as each day you think of your child,
I pray that some peace you will find.

Try not to dwell on his dying day.
The normal ones instead recall.
Remember how he could make you laugh,
or how he liked bossing you all?

Though your precious son wasn't perfect,
his heart you knew was good and kind.
Now God is providing him sweet rest
and the peace he so longed to find.

My heavy grief one day grow lighter,
as the weeks turn to months, then years.
Remember, how much God loves you all.
He'll help you to deal with your tears.

> Jesus provided the perfect example of forgiveness. Like Him, we must strive to make it something we do freely. This applies to forgiving all people from whom you are estranged — the *living **and** those who have passed.* It doesn't matter who was at fault. Clinging to unforgiveness can result in bitterness which poisons one's soul. So, if there are people you have not forgiven, look to the example of Jesus. Mend broken relationships whenever possible, and forgive those that can't be restored. Life is short and forgiveness is freeing for others *and* for you. *Mary Lee*

Avoiding Bitter Grief

God knows our hurts and our tragedies -
those things that bring us to our knees.
He understands our sorrows are real,
and even *old* hurts, we still feel.

Relationships can be hard to do.
Getting them right always takes two.
No, that's not correct — for it takes *three* —
when God's will we both strive to see.

When death interrupts, anger can churn.
Forgiveness then, we still must learn.
We can't change others, though we may try,
but resentment, we can make die.

It isn't easy to let things go,
but forgiveness we still must show.
A Christ-like example shuts down pride
and helps you make anger subside.

From wanting revenge, make a retreat.
Lay your bitterness at His feet.
A sense of relief, God will give you,
and you'll be blessed when this you do.

Who hasn't wondered what Heaven will look like? Such thoughts come more frequently when we're facing difficult health challenges or possibly death. Even if we think of the most beautiful, most serene, most awe-inspiring place we've ever seen, that cannot compare with Heaven. Nevertheless, poets continue to imagine how Heaven may look. This is *my imagining.* May it bless you. *Mary Lee*

What Will Heaven Be Like?

How Heaven will look, I have wondered.
I truly have wanted to know.
Though I've heard a few descriptions ,
in my mind, I still wonder so.

I know God my Father will be there,
and no tears will fall from my eyes.
When one is in God's holy presence,
there will be no sadness or cries.

I'll finally get to meet Jesus
and be wrapped in His warm embrace.
I'll hear Him so gently speak my name
as I look into His kind face.

The Spirit, I then will get to know -
though for so long He has known me
as He guided me along the path
so Heaven I one day could see.

I know there all comfort is waiting.
On a sea of calm, I will rest.
With the saints of old, I'll get to dwell
where we'll be eternally blessed.

With all pains and heartaches forgotten,
joy alone will live in my heart.
With God I will then be forever
where nothing can keep us apart.

ODDS & ENDS:
Memories & A Touch of Humor

In Bible times, travel from place was often difficult as well as dangerous. Having someplace safe and welcoming where one could stop in to eat and rest while traveling was truly a blessing, This is a picture of genuine hospitality. With this poem I've highlights how I frequently experienced such hospitality while I was a part of a military family. The same was true stateside and overseas, and especially among Christians who loved enjoying food and fellowship in one another's homes. When back in the States, the Military and Christian expressions of hospitality continued to be exhibited in homes like that of the Adays, Mareks, Spears, and others, too many to name. It was debatable whether it was the guests or the hosts who found the most blessings from such sharing.

Mary Lee

A Hospitality Home

Some people seem to have the knack,
for they know just how to please.
With their graciousness and kindness,
they help folks feel at ease.

They share their bounty so gladly
when they open wide their door,
At night if all beds are taken,
they'll make pallets on the floor!

Their guests know they're always welcome -
for that's how they make folks feel.
Though sometimes it can be hectic,
they still say, "It's no big deal!"

They honored God with their sharing.
His love, they let others see,
and they've been an inspiration,
to many, including me!

God bless you!

High school reunions are interesting. At early reunions, classmates try to look as successful as possible to impress others. Then as years pass, there is less interest in pretense and more in joy of simply re-connecting. Reunions can be a time for a bit of anxiety as those attending wonder if they'll be the ones who have gained the most weight, lost the most hair, or if they'll even be recognized by others without the aid of name tags. As the number of years from graduation increases, the number of classmates remaining dwindles. By the time our fiftieth rolled around, our number had grown rather small as many of us were then in poor health and others had passed away. Nevertheless, I was happy to be there for our 25th *AND* our 50th! *Mary Lee*

A Time of Remembering
(Written for the Class of '67 on our **25**th Reunion)

We had quite a special weekend
that carried us back in time.
We laughed and shared some memories
that were long stored in each mind.

We mused about the fun-filled days
when youth was in our grasp.
We also shed a tear or two
as we thought of friends now passed.

We smiled to hear our *wild young men*
Who have daughters that now date.
Somehow, it isn't so funny
when they walk the floors and wait!

We *girls* added a pound or two
plus an occasional line,
but we're okay with who we are,
and we like ourselves just fine.

We had fun getting together -
relaxed, with peace in each heart,
grateful that we are *not* eighteen
and about to make our start!

This world's now a different place –
so busy and full of vice.
What happened to those *"Good Old Days"*
when everything seemed so nice?

Lucille Whitworth, a former Post Mistress in Mountain View, Arkansas, was an extraordinary lady. In her mid-60's, she took up painting. Although she was great at it, she didn't call herself an "artist" but rather "just a painter". I commissioned her to do a painting of my dad's old second-hand store. I only had one picture to show her, and the details in it were poor. The painting pictured here was how she *imagined* it might have looked. [Daddy would certainly not have recognized it fori it was *too pretty*!] Lucille was indeed a great artist, but more than this, she was a great Christian lady full of biblical wisdom and positivity. When in her 90's someone would ask her, *"How are you doing today?" She would always reply: "This is the best day of my life!"* May these words inspire us all.   *Mary Lee*

Lucille Whitworth - "Mama Whit"

With her pencils, paints, and her brushes,
   she created each work of art.
Though she claimed, "I'm not a *real artist* —
   just someone who paints from my heart."

Her mind would envisioned an image
   of something she wished to portray.
Then she'd search for just the right colors,
   like poets for right words to say.

She would blend precision with whimsey,
   into painting she would create.
Imaginative and so lovely!
Her paintings folks labeled as "great".

Her attention to detail impressed.
Her desire was to get things right.
For many weeks, she'd sometimes labor,
and she'd work from morning till night.

There was love in her every brush stroke.
Her paintings could make people smile.
Her friends once asked, "Show us how to paint."
so, painting she taught for a while.

Besides Lucille's artistic talent,
God blessed her with others to use.
He gave her wit, wisdom, and kindness,
she used as she chased away blues.

We're thankful for all she shared with us,
her stories as well as her art.
In days ahead she'll be remembered
as someone with God in her heart.

"Ernest Brock's Old Store" Trumann, Arkansas by Mama Whit

Over twenty-five years ago The Church of the Holy Spirit near my home in Memphis planted some small trees in their church yard near the sidewalk. One day as I was walking by, I noticed bronze plaques at the base of each tree and on each was written a different name. After inquiring at the church, I learned their significance which is explained in the poem. The trees and their markers have now been moved toward the back of the property where they have more room to grow. I can't help but wonder if the current congregants know the story of the trees and of the children in whose honor they were planted. *Mary Lee*

Memorial Trees

In the church yard they'd been planted –
small, lovely flowering trees.
Each represented a young life
that illness, then death had seized.

They'd come from far away countries,
each with a story to tell.
They'd hoped to find a miracle
that could help them to get well.

So valiantly each child struggled
holding on as best they could.
When their bodies became so tired,
our loving God understood.

He sent His angels down for them
so with Him they could reside.
Their trees now serve to remind us,
their home is by Jesus' side.

As these trees grow tall in stature,
let's not forget why they're here.
They represent little children
whose lives to God were so dear.

> The following true story had to be included in my first book! I wasn't sure if the young man would allow me to use it since it was a true story about him. I called his grandmother, Lovie, to get permission. She said I could ask him. When he was on the line I read what I had written and waited for his response. Upon asking, can I use it, he gave a resounding YES, and I could almost see him laughing! I then confirmed that I had his permission to include his name. He again agreed. So, thank you, **Aiden Davis**, for this special story and for being such a fine young man!
>
> *"Ms." Mary Lee*

The Nine-Year-Old Negotiator

Vacation Bible School was wrapping up. We'd spent four nights learning stories about four miracles Jesus did during the start of his ministry. I wanted our 9 to 10-year-old class to remember these stories and to understand their significance. So, I printed a sheet with four short memory verses – one for each night's story and passed it out. I then told the children if any of them would come to me within the next two weeks and recite the verses, I would give them a dollar. I realized it was only a dollar, but surely they could use a dollar for something.

Aiden, a very bright and active 9-year-old boy who has always marched to the beat of his own drum, came up to me after I'd announced the offer with the following comment: "Uh, did you know the dollar store has gone up on its prices? Everything there costs a dollar and a quarter now. Could you maybe give us a dollar and a quarter instead of a dollar?"

I almost cracked up, but I managed to reply with a counter offer. I explained there was a short summary verse at the bottom of the page. If they would learn that one too, I would give them a *dollar **and a quarter**.*

Unfortunately, my counter offer was apparently not attractive enough. Neither this young man nor any of the others took me up on it. However, I am sure of one thing: Aiden is going places when he grows up. ***He's already quite a negotiator!***

An Unexpected Blessing

In early 1975, just a few months before my father died from cancer, he asked my mom to promise to do something for him if he wasn't around to do it himself. He knew he didn't have much time, and there were two young boys he wanted to send to Bible camp come summer. As he expected, Daddy died that May. When summer came, Mother fulfilled her promise, and the boys attended Camp Wyldewood, near Searcy, Arkansas.

Years later, in November of 1997, my mom was approached by a man in his thirties whom she did not recognize. He shared the following with her, and she later shared it with me.

"Mrs. Brock, I don't know if you'll remember me, but I wanted to come by and tell you about something that made a profound impact on my life, and it involved your husband, Ernest. When I was just a little kid, I would come with my dad and hang around your store. Mr. Brock was always real nice to me and my brothers. That year while he was still up and around, he asked us if we'd like to go to camp when summer came. We said, 'Yes!' He then said he would see to it we could. That June, after Mr. Brock had passed away, you drove up to our house one day and told us if we still wanted to go to camp, we could. We were thrilled."

"You don't know how much it meant to me to go to camp that summer, Mrs. Brock. It was an experience I'll never forget. I wouldn't have been able to go without what you did. I know I'm a better person today for having gone to camp and for what I learned there. Now I've got kids of my own, and I believe I'm a better daddy because of some of the things I learned that summer thanks to Mr. Brock and you. I just wanted to let you know how much it meant to me and to my family."

As my mom told me about the young man's visit, we both cried. It was to hear such a positive story about Daddy, and although it made us cry, our tears were happy ones because they came from remembering something good he had done to bless those boys' lives.

A few days later, God gave me this poem. I hope it will remind all who read of how we never know the far-reaching impact of a little act of kindness we do for others.   *Mary Lee*

Little Act of Kindness

Those small, simple acts of kindness
can mean so much to another -
even if it is something small
to bless one's sister of brother.

The influence of little deeds,
for many years may ripple on –
long after we have forgotten-
perhaps even after we're gone.

Take every chance to do good deeds.
Opportunities do not miss!
Begin today by reaching out.
Go on now and give it a try!

When you've helped somebody else,
you'll recognize YOU have been blessed!
Then after one act of kindness,
you'll no longer just sit and rest!

For as long as I can recall people have taken pictures of special moments they wish to remember. Presently, most photos are made with our phones and stored in the phone or in the Cloud. In years past, family photos may have been kept in albums, or in boxes, or an old suitcase under the bed. Today many of us can't identify half the people in old pictures, but we know each had a story. I find it sad many of those stories are now lost or left to the imagination of whomever may pull out the box. These are some of my old pictures. *Mary Lee*

MEMORIES AND PHOTOGRAPHS

Wondered why God gave us memories,
and why some remain ever strong?
Some in our minds can play on repeat
like a favorite hymn or song.

While some bring us joy in recalling,
some others we'd like to forget.
This also applies to people whom
we've known for years or just met.

Events we recall through memories -
some are good while others are bad.
The former can bring us happiness.
The latter can make us feel sad.

Our memories can serve a purpose
and prove to be quite useful tools.
When they remind us what *NOT* to do,
they can help us not act like fools.

Preserve your photos and memories.
Learn names and describe the events,
so one day when *your* kids tell *their* kids,
the pictures to them will make sense.

Photos to Treasure

My Parents: Helen &
Ernest Brock
married 1946

Cousins at my
[Mary Lee's] 3rd
birthday March
1952

Pictures tell stories
like freeze-frozen life -
reminders of days now past.

We treasure the memories
they represent, and we want
to make each of them last:

family reunions,
birthday cakes,
holiday meals with a friend,

weddings, anniversaries,
neighborhood kids,
vacations we hoped
wouldn't end.

All were treasures
we wished to hold tight,
for each one to us was dear.

Looking at people
pictured in them, is like
holding loved ones near.

So, when old photos you pull out,
take time to consider each scene.

Do you know why each photo
was kept and
what each one may mean?

Stella & Milton
Parrish's 50th
Anniversary
November 1969

Julia Cash & D.V.
Brock's Wedding
1/18/1903

Part of James & Emma
Parrish Family Reunion
about 1946

1960's—Christmas Dinner at the
Parrish home in the 1960's

Ernest Brock—US
Army WW2
and
Ernie (Curtis) Brock –
USMC, now retired

Certain places have a way of moving us to the core. As a woman of words, I often like to write about my impressions and imaginings related to things I see. This essay came to me after a day of visiting an old Confederate Cemetery in West Helena, Arkansas that dates back to 1869. I visited it with my author friend, Patricia Clark Blake, who was doing research for one of her novels in **The Shiloh Saga**. I hope as you read this you will grasp a bit of the somberness and sense of loss I felt the day we visited it. *Mary Lee*

Heroes Remembered?

An old Civil War Cemetery sits high on a ridge shaded by magnolias and other large trees expected to offer their protective oversight to this resting place of the dead. Years and storms have broken, split, and sometimes up-rooted some of these stalwart sentries as they stood their watch.

On the highest ground a few grand monuments rise skyward - one nearly two stories high. Recorded on all sides of the largest one in both English and Latin, are proclamations affirming how gratitude, praise, and unending regard will be held for the fallen men - heroes who gave their all to a cause the South believed was true and just.

In front of and surrounding the grander monuments, are rows of smaller, slab-like, stone markers, positioned as if they were soldiers in their ranks. Below them lay remains of privates to generals, volunteers and conscripts - soldiers all, who shared a common fate that brought them to this place. Death.

Some markers stand straight and tall like the men whose names they bear. Others lean precariously, with a few even toppled to the ground. Faded lettering on most is nearly illegible. On some, one can make out a name, home state, or perhaps the battle in which death occurred. On others, only the words "Confederate Dead" are found.

On this hilltop, the once thunderous rumblings from the big guns in the fort below are now silent. Stillness hangs heavily like the drooping branches of the trees. Heard are neither the screams from war terrors, nor the quiet sobbing of battle-weary men as they lie dying, sometimes calling for their mother or sweetheart. Tears of mourners are no longer shed on this hilltop tomb, nor the voices of fine orators who once passionately prophesied of imminent victories. Perhaps some of those very speakers lie sleeping in grass-covered beds here or in a nearby cemetery.

Now, over one hundred and fifty years removed, visitors seldom come to disturb the quietness of this sad sanctuary. No one seems interested in reading names of men, towns, states, or battles fought in, nor in recounting the deeds of daring the fallen wrought in generations past. Here forlorn and forgotten, neither markers of stone, granite, or marble can truly ensure the memory of the dead will endure for these warriors of the past. Quite a sobering thought to ponder on a beautiful summer day.

Fun with Dad's Old Wagon

The once red wagon rested on its end, just outside the grandmother's garage. It was placed in this position to help prevent rain from collecting inside and causing it to rust even more than it already had. The wagon was about forty-years old at the time, not an antique one would deem of much value in the marketplace. It certainly wasn't the shiny ride it once had been. Indeed, many years had passed since it was involved in play. Once its boy had grown too big to want to be pulled about in it, the wagon had become little more than a yard tool.

In its new life, the old wagon was called into duty for hauling. It carried brush and bags of leaves to the curb, or it carted bags of potting soil or flowers to beds for planting. It proved easier for the grandmother to use than a wheelbarrow since the wagon didn't have to be balanced. She was glad she had kept it.

One fall day when two of her young grandsons were visiting from out of town the grandmother, thought of something the boys might find entertaining. She would show them how they could have some fun with the old wagon. Since her house was built on the side of a hill, her driveway had a fairly steep slope. If someone sat in the wagon, and it was given a slight push from the top of the drive, it would speedily descend the curved drive, providing quite a thrill for whoever was riding inside it! Now all the boys needed was to see a demonstration, and who was there to provide it besides their grandmother, MeeMee?

At first, they weren't convinced this was something

they wanted to try. Also, they were a bit fearful they would not be able to steer the wagon as it began its downhill flight. The only thing to do was for their grandmother to make the ride with the boys. So, one-at-a-time, she would do just that.

Before the rides could begin, MeeMee she had to get into the wagon herself. This required positioning her ample backside into the rear bed of the wagon - *not an easy task*! Next, she had to wedge a grandson into the front of the wagon, between her outstretched legs. Then she had to hold the wagon's tongue firmly in her hands for steering. Whichever boy wasn't riding got the honor of giving the wagon a push.

It was now time to ride. Down the driveway, the unlikely duo sped with shouts of laughter abounding! "Next—I want to go next!" was heard from each grandson as they clamored for a turn.

For quite some time, the boys took turns riding with their grandmother, then with one another. They didn't seem to mind having to pull the wagon back up the steep driveway after each ride because they knew what came next —a fun-filled flight back down! If it were possible, the old wagon itself would probably have been expelling shrieks of joy that day for once more it was getting to play!

MeeMee's NOTE:
I can't recall who I got to take this photo, but I am so glad I still had it to document the joyful faces we all wore that fun, fall day!

> *Like people, pets die, and when they do they leave an unforgettable hole in our hearts. The following poem is a Memorial Tribute to my last dog, Mowgli. Over the years I have been commissioned to do this for other people who have also lost their beloved pets. The process of writing it for me was cathartic. When I've done one for other people, they have said it helped them with their grief because it honored their pet who had brought so much love into their homes and lives.*   *Mary Lee*

He's Running in Heaven

My heart is filled with sadness and grief.
Today I told Mowgli 'Goodbye'.
Though we've been family for nine plus years,
I'm amazed how the time did fly.

When we rescued Mowg from the shelter,
he was just a scared little pup.
His size was so tiny way back then,
he'd fit in a big coffee cup.

Caleb had wanted him for his dog,
but it didn't take long to see,
this spotted puppy had become mine,
and for all of his life, he'd be.

When Mowgli went through his chewing stage
on some antiques he left his mark.
I said at the time, "I'll kill that dog!"
but my bite didn't match my bark.

When Mowgli and Noah were quite young,
lots of funny things we'd get to see -
like a boy walking 'round on all fours
so that like his Mowgli he'd be!

MOWGLI CUNNINGHAM
??? — 12/7/2010

Cole came along and loved Mowgli, too.
No doubt Ian would have as well,
and if they'd had more time together,
their stories of Mowg they would tell.

For *MeeMee Mary*, Mowg's loss was great
since he often slept in her bed.
Many the morning his bark told her,
"Get up, Mom, I need to be fed!"

Though Mowg became a great inside dog,
he clearly was born to run!
When free, he tore through the neighborhood.
Once home, he'd collapse from the fun.

We truly will miss our Mowgli,
for he brought us joy every day.
If for dogs there's a place in heaven,
that is where we hope Mowg will stay.

For now we'll remember the good times.
Let's not sit around being sad.
We were blessed for a while with Mowgli,
and our time with him made us glad.

Many of you reading this book are familiar with Sarah Young's devotional book, Jesus Calling. Some of you who are mothers of small children may even have a copy in a bathroom book rack because that is the only place in your home where you can find a few moments of peace and quiet to think, read, or pray. One thing I loved about Jesus Calling is there is a version that provides space in which you can write your responses or thoughts as promoted by the day's devotional or the accompanying scriptures. Often, my responses came out as a poem. One of these is printed below. The main thing I would like readers to take away from this is God is not put off by **where** we happen to pray as long as we come to Him humbly and respectfully - even if it is in "The Potty". *Mary Lee*

Delighting in My Lord EVERYWHERE

Please give me the eyes to see
so, I'm open to Your will,
and with Your very Spirit,
may all of my life You fill.

I want to bring You honor
as these thoughts I pause to pen.
God, when You're moving in me,
it is easy to begin.

Perhaps if someone reads this
when they are needing a lift,
in it they may find a blessing
because I have used Your gift.

Written 11-28-22 in response to Jesus Calling's daily devotional.

> When a friend is celebrating her milestone **30th birthday**, *and she is a 'ringer'* for Barbie, the card you give her must be funny. This poem was written for my friend, Kim Ryan, manager of a Jenny Craig Weight Loss Center in Memphis where I once worked. When I read the poem to her, she was a good sport and laughed along with the whole staff. The funny thing is **that** was back in the **1990's**, and she is **still a beauty today**!
> *Mary Lee*

Welcome To *Middle Age*!

Today our sweet friend has turned 30,
but 30's not really so old –
when compared to wine or a fine cheese,
(or other things covered with mold!)

It's okay she's not yet married.
Some single guys still are around,
and a few even have their own hair,
(though not lots of them can be found.)

But it's not just she who is aging,
for <u>Barbie</u> is older now, too.
Of course, Barbie's figure's not sagging.
(With plastic, so much they can do!

We hope that she's really not bothered
by all of this focus on age.
If she'll think of life as a novel.
(True — she <u>is</u> getting near the last page!)

Yet when today's party is over,
we friends, really do want to say,
Precious Kim, you're just getting better!
Hope you'll have a *HAPPY BIRTHDAY*!

> The following little piece is a remembrance from my youth. It recounts a trip my family and I made one summer in the 1960's. On the way back from a short vacation, we came through Hardy, Arkansas, which provided the setting for the following "math lesson". *Mary Lee*

A Mathematical Riddle:
[How can 1 + 1 = 2, yet 2 + 1 = 1]

It was near the end of a most pleasant day.
My little brother and I had been begging
to wade in one of the nice streams
we saw running along beside the road.
Finally, our mother gave in,
and dad pulled the car over,
not far from a nearby campground.

When he had stopped, my little brother and I
threw open the car's back doors
and made a dash for the stream.
The water was cool and inviting
as we splashed and laughed
UNTIL
something slithered beside us
in the water
Yikes! A snake!

Even more quickly than we'd gotten out of the car,
we were climbing back inside!

We discovered this new math fact that day:

1 + 1 = 2 in the water
BUT
2 + 1 does *NOT* = 3 in the water

(if 1 = *a slithering, snake!)*

Some days a girl just needs to laugh a bit at herself and her situation. As a single lady, I was the person responsible for mowing my lawn. Writing this made me smile. Hope you'll smile, too.
Mary Lee

'Ode' to Mowing
[after coming inside "sweaty hot"]

I stand here in my all together,
and I'm thankful as I can be
that shades on my windows were pulled down
so my neighbors couldn't see me.

My head, neck and face I promptly doused
with the hose in my kitchrn sink.
I'm glad it's just the dog and me here
because I am sure that I stink!

Once I had cooled down and caught my breath,
a cold shower would hit the spot.
I think in my rush to get it done,
I *almost* had gotten too hot!

For sure, if I buy another home,
a much smaller lawn I will find.
Though it might mean I'd scoop more poop then,
I really don't think I will mind.

If on a hill, I'll have terraces,
with easy-care shrubs and flowers –
instead of the ones I have to weed
that each week take hours and hours.

Or maybe I'll hire a strong yardman -
a young one with muscles galore!
Then I can sit back and watch him work!
That surely would *not* be a chore!

Till then the mowing is up to me
to keep the grass under control.
At least there's one thing I learned today:
it looks like I've chased off the mole!

> You know your mate better than anyone else. If humor floats his boat, perhaps he would enjoy this poem next Valentine's Day! Copy it into a neat blank card so he can treasure it always. [**However**, it wouldn't be a bad idea if you sweeten the deal by including in the card a couple of tickets to a special event he's been wanting to see!] ☺   *Mary Lee*

A "Not-So-Serious" Valentine

Happy Valentine's Day, dear Sweetheart -
the man whom I never would trade -
not even for someone like Brad Pitt!
[Too long in the sun have I stayed?]

You make me feel I'm important
with the things that you **let** me do -
like **letting** me take out the garbage
[when it's been forgotten by you!]

Or **letting** me balance the checkbook -
when debits you didn't record;
or **letting me** get a 'new' table.
[It may look good once it's restored.]

Yes, your heart overflows with kindness.
From your lips, the "**sweet nothings**" pass:
"I found nothing wrong with your gas gauge."
[Then why did I run out of gas!]

The party you said was "casual",
though the invite had said **black tie**!
Then we arrived in casual clothes!
[I felt like I wanted to die!]

But we've made it this far together,
and it's really not been *TOO BAD*!
I'll still keep you as my Valentine.
♥Now, doesn't that make you feel glad?♥

Our pets are such a blessing and we love them. They bring us so much joy, even though they can at times be quite demanding. Princess came to me as a stray back in 2012. When she planted herself on my deck that summer and started meowing I thought she was hungry, so I fed her. *[As a life-long dog person, I didn't know what that meant!]* I had *unintentio*nally become a cat owner! I wrote this poem about Princess for my young friend, Jillian Scroggins, who also loves my cat, even though her allergies don't like cat fur!   *Mary Lee*

PRINCESS:
My Furry Alarm Clock

Though I did not wish to leave my nice bed,
Princess kept jumping over my head!

The sun had risen, but I closed my eyes.
Just a little more sleep, I would prize.

Yet, once on my bed, she began to purr,
but she'd lie still if I stroked her fur.

Her stillness lasted but for a short while.
She'd made me get up, and I would smile.

That's just how it is **when a cat owns you**.
There's nothing for them you wouldn't do.

Isn't it great to share food with friends? You get to enjoy dishes you might never have made for yourself. My best friend, Sanet Jennings, and I are always sharing food with other people and with one another, especially soups. The specific recipe mentioned below I would not share with **anyone** but her. You'll understand why when you've read the poem.   *Mary Lee*

Anyone Up for Soup?

My friend and I are soup-making queens,
and we love making it to share!
Even when batches are rather small,
we'll usually have soup to spare.

One day I tried to concoct a soup
that would have a nice Asian taste.
With some chicken broth, I started out
then in the pot veggies I placed.

It had to include some fresh snow peas,
yet one thing I knew I must do —
remove the strings from each little pod,
or the soup I would have to chew!

Diligently, I then went to work,
so that I could remove each string.
I was determined to get them all,
if not, a **soup fail** this would bring.

With spices added, it smelled so good.
I was glad I'd made a large pot.
A spoonful said the flavor was great,
but there was one thing that was **not!**

Somehow the peas still seemed to have strings!
This caused me to chew and to chew.
Rather than swallow, I spit them out.
It was all that I knew to do.

Now, what could be done with so much soup?
Just thinking of this made me smile.
I called my friend: "I'm bringing you soup,
and I'll be there in a short while."

Arriving, I handed her a spoon,
"It's tasty but spit out the string!
I know just what I should call this soup —
and it has a familiar ring."

"**Spit Soup**" of course is a perfect fit,
but "**Floss Soup**" is the name I gave.
Someone could eat and floss all at once,
just think of the time you could save!

[Hum: I asked my dentist, Dr.Cook, if he'd
like for me to whip up a pot for him,
but I've gotten no reply yet.]

When a good friend with a particularly dry wit is having a birthday, a funny poem is sure to fit the occasion. This poem I wrote nearly thirty years ago to share with a dear friend, John Marek, Sr. When I was selecting pieces to go in this book, I called his widow, Pat, and asked her if I should include it. I read it to her over the phone and both of us laughed as we remembered that party many years ago. We spoke of John's sense of humor and that sly little grin he would sometimes get on his face. We agreed that John would be pleased if I used it. How blessed we are when we can remember fun times and laughter shared with friends, including those now departed. *Mary Lee*

Happy Thoughts on Your 51st Birthday

Well, I've heard you're one year older,
but really, I just can't tell.
Ain't it great that Grecian Gel
covers grey so dog-gone well?

Of course, there are the new glasses
we see that these days you need.
They make you look so dignified.
What a pity you can't read!

But your smile is just as winning
as it was a few years back,
and your dentures slip so seldom.
For wearing them, you've a knack!

Some may say you are **over the hill**,
but John, we know that's not true.
We think you went **around** it, friend,
for that's so much more like you!

Enjoy your 51st birthday,
and always keep in mind,
the rest of us may be younger,
but we aren't that far behind!

Happy Birthday to John -
One Cool Dude
& Many Happy Returns! *

* (Maybe some of the stuff you get will be worth keeping!)

This book,
like summer,
has come to an end.
I hope you have been
blessed by what you've read.
Look for more poetry from me
coming your way in 2025!

Mary Lee

ABOUT THE AUTHOR

Mary Lee Cunningham is a writer of verse which flows from her pen as freely as water flows from a mountain stream. She has written essays, articles, and devotionals, some of which have previously been published. Many of her poems also appear in her custom greeting cards, "Expressions from the Heart".

Mary Lee's academic background includes a B.A. in Communications [Speech] and an M.A. in Marriage and Family Counseling – *earned thirty-four years apart* – from Harding University. Further influences on her writing stem from her past work experiences: time spent as a military wife; five and a half years as a classroom teacher; decades as a student of God's Word; and a frequent teacher for ladies' classes.

Evidence of a strong Christian faith runs throughout Mary Lee's writing. She considers as her greatest compliment something contained in a thank-you note she once received for a poem she wrote for a family who had lost a child. In the note, the family called her a sweet "psalmist".

Mary Lee, formerly from Memphis, Tennessee, now resides in Jonesboro, Arkansas—the city where she was born and seventeen miles from Trumann, Arkansas where she grew up. She is the mother of one son and a grandmother to three fine grandsons.

www.ingramcontent.com/pod-product-compliance
Lightning Source LLC
LaVergne TN
LVHW021119080426
835510LV00012B/1759